THINK

BY NADIA OHAR

Published by Starry Night Publishing.Com

Rochester, New York

Copyright 2016 Nadia Ohar

Nadia Ohar

Contents

Nadia Ohar

PREFACE

"I had everything wrong!"

"No, you had everything right. Without opposition you would not be able to understand choices. You see, in a system where nothing seems perfect, you need both, the appearance of right and wrong, so you can make a conscious choice. These choices will bring you to another level in your life. You really can't make a wrong decision because any choice you make will continue to direct you to your highest good."

"If I go back and tell everyone about this place, no one is going to believe me!"

"Let me ask you this: If you approached mankind and they were not aware they started out as an egg that was fertilized by sperm and would grow in a woman's stomach whereas nine months later, they would transition into the world via the magnificent body tunnel that brings them into the light…do you think they would listen? So if that absurdness is all real and hardly believable, then surely this Spirit World can be understood. This is really where it all begins. You will be named, assigned, and like so many others, will go forth with your gifts. Directions will be stamped on the palms of your hands and no other being will have the same exact mapping as anyone else. While you are here, in the Spirit World, there is a continuous flow of learning that takes place. It is here, you will be given your mission to go when the One Source calls you by your assigned name. For now, as Spirit, you are absorbing information, studying your script, and proceeding forward to the tunnel that will transition you to your temporary destination. The mission is short, a lifetime at best, but it is yours to do with as you choose. I want to praise many of you on your successes, completing your mission as instructed, by helping others to move from "scarcity" to abundant living. The responsible choices you all made took courage and your efforts were commendable. Now, it is in this timing, that we are faced with still another dilemma that needs your service and even more courage to turn violence into peace and turmoil into harmony. Fear is prominent in the world where you will be descending to shortly and your mission will be to raise the consciousness level to the vibration of truth which will be no easy task. You will dissipate darkness by bringing your light forth, not by judging, but by acceptance. You will develop courage and strength, not by casting a stone, but by leaving the gift of love at every doorstep and threshold you cross. Responding in this way, your enemies will know there is another way. I leave this mission open to volunteers. The great Master is here and He will guide you forth. All volunteers are present except one..."

"You, the one lingering by yourself, please come forward. You are in need of forgiveness?"

"Yes my Master. I failed my mission before and I fear I would fail again."

"Tell me how you believe you failed."

"I was very angry with my Mother and Father and rebelled against them. I did not honor them."

"Was it in your heart to make them suffer?"

"Oh No Lord, I was self-centered and afraid that I would not get my way."

"So you were afraid and filled with fear?"

"Yes Master, so very afraid."

"This does not sound like a malicious heart."

"But Master, in my marriage, I had an affair. I committed adultery!"

"Tell me about this marriage. Were you happy?"

"No. We fought all the time and nothing I did seemed to please him and he was very unhappy too."

"Were you the cause of his unhappiness?"

"I think not but maybe there was something I could have done different to make him happy."

"If you were not the cause of his unhappiness, then surely you were not the solution."

"But my affair!!!"

"Of course...you thought this other person was your solution, but if he was not the cause of your unhappiness, he was not your solution either."

"Forgive me Master, but it seems like I did everything wrong the last time I volunteered to make a difference and I think I would not be of service to anyone on the planet with my lack of understanding."

"My most promising Spirit, you first have to understand that you descended into a system where nothing seemed perfect and in order to have what appeared to be right, you had to have circumstances that appeared to be wrong because you need comparisons in order to make choices. It's in these choices that help you grow into the being I created you to be." This is why "forgiveness" is necessary and judgments of others are to be discerned properly. Your mission will be to help others through their choices by giving unconditional love, the same way I give to you, through all circumstances.... There is one more choice you made that I would like to see you re-evaluate."

"What is that Master?"

"The last time you were sent with a gift. Do you remember what that gift was?"

"Yes, it was the gift of writing and discernment."

"Why do you think you placed it aside?"

"I was so busy judging and feeling guilty about being wrong that I didn't think I had the right to use my gift."

"And now?"

"I am understanding the power of forgiveness and the importance of using my gifts as I am assigned."

"Now that you have learned from past choices, and are ready to move forward, I will name you so you may go forth and use your gift to make a difference in the world. You will not be alone as you will occupy a body in which to view life's happening on Earth. This body will have a brain and many times you will be challenged by this remarkable organ that is programmed with information, some of which is camouflaged in lies. This brain can justify, distort reality and knock you off balance with intellectual data unless you stay grounded in truth. This time use your brain, not as your enemy, but embrace it as a friend and it can work with you instead of against you, much the same way you will be asked to embrace your enemy in order to participate in forgiveness and love. This time you will replace fear with faith in the goodness of life and allow your Spirit to guide you in your most challenging endeavors now that you know you have a choice. Choice and conscious living is the only difference between making a better life and creating a ripple effect that touches the lives of others. The path may be long and narrow and if you should veer off course, rest assured, you will receive signs to confirm your location. Now it is time to be reborn. Go forth and use your gifts wisely to help others on their journey to evolve into a higher understanding of truth. You will be the Word Whisperer. It's your choice."

CHAPTER ONE

"EARth hears your words…listen closely to your demands;
Your world is filled with thoughts, and all your commands…"

Word Whisperer

Here I sit at my computer, with the nagging desire to write another book but not just any book. This one has to be the "be all"…end all…you know something that is different but on the other hand makes sense after all…..Everything I have done in my life has always been a little different. As I look back on my life, I see that growing up as a middle child of four other siblings wasn't always easy. Or maybe it was easy because I had people around me that would try and make things easy for me so that I really didn't have to do too much for myself. I lost my Mother when I was twelve years old, unexpectedly, and that loss has stayed with me throughout my life. I decided that I never wanted to experience that kind of pain ever again so that took care of getting really close to anyone in my life. I picked a marriage partner that made it easy to stay distant and decided to have four children because that gave me a sense of purpose and I could lose myself in their lives trying to decide what would be best for them. How many of you know that kids grow and you are left with yourself once again? Well that is exactly what happened to me. I tried to make my life about my children because it seemed easier to take the focus off myself. If I could tend to someone's needs, I didn't have to figure out my own needs because that would mean I'd have to take responsibility for creating a life of my dreams and I just didn't know how to do that. Then the grand kids came and once again I had purpose…and once again they grew and their needs got smaller and smaller. So now I sit facing a computer and listening to the still voice inside of me that says "it's time!!!!"

I must say I have always experienced a deeper meaning to life than most. I had the need to understand why something was said or why something was happening. My life always had a 3-D effect and I loved the idea that "Life is an adventure!" When I am writing, I even look closely at the letters that form words and see them as "little entities" of their own…that each letter has meaning For instance, in the word "life" the letter "i" stands out for me because "I" am at the center of life. Now you might notice that the word "word" has the word "or" in it, because some words can mean this "OR" that. Not always the same thing.

The purpose of this book is not to pick words apart but find deeper meaning to life. Words do have a purpose and they have the power to influence and shape our lives…I do notice the word "power" has the letters "OW" which means we can use our power to hurt or to join together in unison as a "we" which is also located in the word "power." Okay, I will move on…but I just want you to realize that everything is closely related and has meaning. The words you are reading are made of letters combined using the same letters over and over again but in different formation. We are similar to these letters because we all have the same body parts but we are formatted to make different lives for ourselves… same parts…different meanings. What a difference one letter can make in a word. What a difference one person can make in the world. While I am on the subject of words and meanings it has come to my attention that the word "exist" is closely related to the word "exit" and are both closely connected. First we exist, and then we exit this world. Because I have to seek more meaning to this process, I started to really think on the subject of dying and the real meaning behind it. The easiest way to try and understand this concept is to bring it back to when you were already dead, before you were born. Now, I find there is no fear when I think about when I wasn't here before, so I have to believe there is nothing to fear about leaving here to that place of "not existing" once again. Even when we go to sleep at night, we have to "let go' in order to get rest and we have no idea where we go, so to speak. I don't see any fear in falling to sleep. Feeling like I don't have a choice in the matter of death, I want to make it as comfortable as possible for this re-birth to take place. Now women, who have birthed children know how important it is to find a way to go through the process of child birth with the least amount of pain during this time. Whether by breathing techniques or with the help of drugs, or natural, it still can be a painful process to go through. I believe that we are all in the womb of the Universe right now, and we will be birthed into another life eventually. Some of us are pre-mature, some of us are aborted, miscarried, and some of us are full term. In any case, there will be a birth canal to leave here. The Universe will birth us back to the invisible.

I used to wonder why our bodies had to grow old and refuse to carry us like it once did, but now I understand part of the process. You see, if we didn't change at all, none of us would want to leave here and that is not our destiny. Sometimes we create sickness or other painful ailments, so that we can participate in the process of "letting go" so we can continue on to our next destination. It would be harder to leave if there was no pain involved. Yes, pain carries us to another place but remember pain brought us here too. So instead of blaming God, the Universe or whatever is responsible for our existence, start being grateful and thankful for your precious lives so you may enjoy your time while existing on this planet.

Sometimes we shed tears of joy for the birth of a child because we are celebrating new beginnings. Our loved ones pass into new beginnings through the passage of death. We also shed tears once again. There is no other way to get here and no other way to leave except through the passage of birth and death. When a baby is born, it comes to Earth with a pure Spirit that is reflected by the love of everyone who comes in contact with this baby. The Spirit stays pure and cannot tarnish and is here to direct us if we would only listen. However, as this child grows and takes on lessons that might distort his or her character, choices are made and vibrations are lowered. We are like magnets and attract into our experiences only at the level we are vibrating at. The Spirit stays pure and is unaffected by the "outer" being. The Spirit is never the thing of itself doing harm but is the connection between this world and the next. Now you might not be comfortable believing that the Spirit of a murderer might go to the same place as that of the Saint, but remember, the Spirit came here pure and it leaves here void of any connection to negative vibrations. That is why we have cause and effect here on Earth. You make a choice and your consequence follows. This is why we don't need punishment in the after-life because we experience everything we put out here in the world. We don't have to be judged twice because it is already taken care of through cause and effect.

When you make a choice, you automatically have the consequence of that choice so if it's something that doesn't feel right, you experience the effect of that result. No one has to tell you how wrong you are because you already know. Sometimes punishment gets in the way of learning the lesson because now the person being punished is putting their energy on the punisher and not on the lesson that comes naturally with choices. Some parents believe that if they don't punish their children, their child will do the same deed again, but the truth is, your child does not want to feel badly about their choices because the Spirit within carries the truth that no man can escape.

Speaking of Spirit, when a loved one passes on, I believe you can connect with them because everything here on Earth carries a certain vibration. We can raise our vibration by prayer, meditation, and quieting our minds. Dreams are another way we can receive messages and thoughts from our loved ones as needed. God is the highest frequency so when we connect with this source, we automatically raise our vibration level. Our Spirit has a vibration of its own which is at a higher frequency than what we are used to within our bodies. Sometimes the Spirit of your loved one can come through in the form of a butterfly, the sound of a wind chime, light, or some other sign that matches their vibration. It is easier for them to connect with something that does not carry baggage that would lower the frequency. Because we are not familiar with the "new way" of communicating, we may feel the absence of the physical presence of our loved one and ultimately we experience feelings of the loss at hand. Any time there is a change or a shift in energy, there is a releasing of emotions. When we bring God into any situation, it helps to lessen the pain we are going through. Knowing that God's love is unconditional, we know that life here on Earth is just a temporary learning station, to teach us how to love each other through life's lessons, until we move to a better place, without all the baggage. Knowing we will meet again does not lessen the pain we feel now. However, it is a bridge to restoring one's self back to its natural state. I have a relationship with God energy daily, by meditating and consciously deciding to connect with the Spiritual side of life. I have never seen the physical presence of Source, but I do believe that Source is real. Whether this is brought forth through thoughts which carry energy, the result is a higher consciousness which produces higher results. If Source is brought into this realm through faith, understanding and prayer, then the place where our loved one now resides is just as real. We don't have to wait until we pass on to share our thoughts and feelings with them. Our bodies change form, but our Spirits remain connected. All of us carry a Spirit within our natural body that will be released in our own passing. Our bodies are merely vehicles to carry our Spirit through experiences on this Earth. When a chicken lays an egg, the egg is just the vehicle for the inside life, but once the chick is ready to come out, the egg changes form and the chick appears. The egg is no longer needed at this time, as is true for the body when we release the Spirit, but never-the-less, the egg served its purpose. In knowing that death is a new beginning, we can give ourselves permission to "let go" and allow the Spirit to descend to greater heights without the complication of holding on to something that needs releasing. In order to celebrate death, we need to have an understanding of the place where our loved ones now reside. I believe that because the Spirit comes from a place of perfection, love and truth, it would stand to reason they would have to venture to a place that matches that goodness. God gives us a Spirit here on Earth because perfection can only be found in the Spirit, not in ourselves as humans. All our imperfections die with the body and the perfect Spirit moves on without issues. It is no longer limited or held back from its perfection by earthly needs and demands. By letting go, we no longer hinder the Spirit, but we celebrate the freedom for our loved ones. As we cleanse all our thoughts of negativity, we bring ourselves closer to that form of perfection that is necessary to communicate effectively with our loved ones. In our joyous state of mind, we are even closer to experiencing the Spirit of our dearly beloved. In prayer or meditation, we bring ourselves to a place of cleansing and releasing, and we glimpse a portion of the Spirit World that will one day be our home too.

Nadia Ohar

THIS THING CALLED LIFE

"HA"piness starts with a smile. "

Word Whisperer

I heard a wonderful quote today stating that the word "smile." stands for "Start My Internal Love Engine." What a wonderful way to start the day. When we get dressed we should all remember to "put on" a smile as well, regardless of whether our feelings match that particular mood. We might not want to get dressed but we certainly are not going out into the world without clothes, so wear the smile and the feelings that match happiness will soon take place. If you "pretend" to be in a good mood, you might experience the good mood. Try this same technique in forgiving someone that seems hard to forgive. Pretend to forgive them and watch the healing take place, not only in your body, but in your heart. It's like stepping into a dark room and carrying a light and pretending that the room is still going to stay dark. It can't happen….so just "fake it till you make it." And you will make it!!!!

I believe we have to stand up to "Fear," which by the way has the word "ear" in it, meaning that fear is created by something you are hearing or something you previously heard in your life. "Hearing" has the word "ear" also for a reason. Okay, back to the point I want to make from all this, which is the way to alleviate fear in your life is by putting your ears to everything that has to do with love. Love carries no fear or any other negative qualities so when you fill yourself with love, loving people, loving words, you are participating in healthy living. By the way, the word "love" is actually spelled "evol backwards and then connects back to the "e" to start over again…for the word "evolve," which is exactly what we are doing here on Earth. It's interesting how one four letter word can have so many meanings in life. Some people equate "love" with sacrifice and killings, others with "conditions," such as you act this way and I will give you my love, otherwise I will disapprove and you will feel the agony of my wrath. "Tough Love" really developed from the lack of healthy love to begin with. If the

15

relationship got to the place where you have to use "tough love," then I would insist on calling it something else. If "tough love" has to be used, than "unconditional" was absent in the first place. "Tough love" is just a protective mechanism for the one performing this act. These relationships take longer to repair. Then there is the avoidance of love attached to pain and rejection of the past, like "love" is something to avoid or is measured out in small quantities. There is the love from God which is supposed to be unconditional, but He is sometimes portrayed as a "tricky God," or a God that holds judgment over all your actions and decides if you are worthy, which by the way, there are actually teachings that tell you that you are not worthy. Try overcoming that in your lifetime, especially if you participate in that ritual all the time. So now you might see why you invite fear in as a guest in your home because you might not get the full meaning of love, the way it was intended to be here on Earth. What about the statement "Love hurts?" I wouldn't be attracted to something that creates pain but the truth is, "love" doesn't hurt. "Bad treatment" hurts. Rejection hurts. Unavailability hurts. Not love!

Before I explain my definition of "love," I want to say that we all assign meaning to people, places, and things. We have a perception of how things are. But what happens when your meaning and my meaning do not match... Now we are involved in who's right and who's wrong....which is called the "win – lose" syndrome. This stems from a pattern of "I know better than you" which constitutes the "competition" in relationships and produces a lack of respect. No one taught you that your opinion has value as well as the next person's opinion. You will see this pattern in politics and religion as well as in your own personal relationships. "Telling" rather than two way communication is damaging to relationships. Parents, it's important to have a two way conversation with your children to give them a sense of worth, and not push your opinions on them so they can be duplicates of you. Otherwise you create insecurities that take years to repair by self-help techniques because one way conversations create anger, frustration, rebellion, and most of all, separation. Did you ever notice that the more people want to be right, the louder their voice becomes? Like noise determines the amount of "rightness." This is especially true in marriages when one person tries to be more right than the other person. Communication requires a speaker and a listener; not two people talking at the same time. You might as well save your breath if you don't have someone listening to you when you speak. By the same token, you give the listener a chance to speak and you become the one who listens.

I don't understand why people think someone has to agree with them in order to give value to what they believe. You can be the only one in the crowd who thinks a certain way and you don't have to get the approval of someone else in order to feel good about what you have to say. That is a form of "people pleasing," trying to say what someone else wants to hear, and that is just not honest. You will lose yourself faster than a speeding bullet if you don't get honest and speak your mind and not the mind of others. I'm sure you've heard the statement "The ones that matter don't mind, and the ones that mind don't matter."

Then there is the subject of "lies" and "dishonesty." Because you don't understand that words are energy, and that dishonesty carries a low vibration, your life will match that vibration and you can't understand why things don't work for you and why your life looks the way it does. It is so easy to justify dishonesty. You call in sick to work when you are well, you cheat on your taxes because you think you come out ahead and who does it really hurt? YOU! It hurts YOU! You only allow goodness in according to your beliefs about yourself. If you know you are a liar, the rewards are few. And what about angry people who tell you not to lie to them but get furious when they don't hear what they want to hear? They profess to want to hear the truth but their reaction to the truth makes them a liar. The very thing they say they want, they reject. This is especially true of parents who tend to be controlling of their children. They are so set on having things be the way they want them, that they demand to hear what they believe would make them happy. They are manipulators and very self-centered and they help their children to become liars and pass on the same pattern. Angry people also tend to hook up with people who seem "weaker" so they can build themselves up as 'superior" and do not participate in "win-win" situations. They lean toward being the ones that need to be right at all costs. They are just playing out the hurts of their past, and until they get to a place of forgiveness for the ones that acted the same way to them, it will remain the same.

Yes, pain has a place in our lives but sometimes we have to know when to "let go." Funny how you think you are avoiding pain by not dealing with it, but the truth is, you are entertaining pain every day and inviting the friends of pain into your life, which happen to be distrust, isolation, anger, unforgiveness, cancer, migraines and other sicknesses. You know who you hang with and you know who you are. I have to say I was one of them…you know, judgmental, knowing best, fighting for superiority, better than… and had to experience the repercussions of my lack of love to myself and others.

What helped me turn my life around was when a small magazine called "Science of Mind" appeared in my life. This was over 35 years ago and I still participate with their philosophy. When I first read articles on non-judgment, I could feel the lightness in my body and how free I felt experiencing harmony and peace. I wanted more of this and I was introduced to Louise Hay's book "You Can Heal Your Life" which contained information on healing past hurts and affirmations that would heal mental causes to health issues. I was truly blessed to continue on my spiritual journey by reading self-help books, watching certain TV shows as well as working with personalized affirmations. I do believe when we are ready to heal, and are open to ideas and methods, the Universe, God, Higher Power, Divine, or whatever Spiritual Method or Being you are connected to, will bring you what you need to heal at the right time.

JUDGEMENTS

Even in the dark there is room for the light;
If you think you are wrong you could be right;
When you drink from the glass that is half empty;
Put it back down until you see that it's plenty....

Word Whisperer

I think what really helped me immensely, to free my spirit to living fully, was letting go of judgment. I don't think you can live fully in love if you make unnecessary judgments which hold you back from having what you say you want. I want to share a blog I wrote recently on:

Opinions versus Judgments:

Did you know that when you walk around judging other people, you are really seeing the same qualities in yourself without realizing it? It is just mirrored back to you, but, because the focus is on the other person, you don't even realize that your comments pertain to yourself. Judgments start in the invisible and are brought to life by thinking thoughts about somebody or some incident. It is necessary to have opinions, but judgments are usually something we "hold on' to for a long period of time. Anything you hold onto takes space and when that space is filled there is no way anything else can enter. There is no room for the good coming your way. Did you notice there are some people who walk around saying they are sorry all the time? They are the ones that are the quickest to judge themselves as being wrong or at fault for something. These judgments keep them in bondage and block their good from getting in. Again, we do live in a world where it seems like we have to judge something to have an opinion, but an opinion does not get stuck in a "holding cell." It merely comes and goes. Observation is healthy but judgment comes from thinking you know best about a particular situation. You seem to have all the answers and you know how it "should be." You think you have the right recipe in life. But what you might not understand is there are many cooks out there that like to make their cake a little different than yours. Just because their ingredients are not the same as yours, doesn't mean their lives are less important in the big kitchen of the world. In other words, some people wear aprons and some do not but that apron or cover up doesn't make you who you are. It's not the appearance as much as it is the utensils you work with. Okay out of the kitchen and into the "living" room of life. You might look out your window and see a big oak tree. You might not realize that giant oak started out as a tiny acorn and transformed into a beautiful tree. This acorn had the ability to grow into something so magnificent because it didn't have any judgments placed upon it. It was able to become what it was supposed to be. We are the same as the acorn. Everything we need to grow into the magnificent being that we are is already placed within us. The only thing that hinders our growth is the judgments put upon us by ourselves and others. We have to learn how to be. I heard it once said that a seed would pray away the dirt if it could, but it is the dirt that is the necessary womb for the seed to grow. So don't think that some of the "dirt" you may encounter in your life is not for your growing experience. When you judge something or someone as "bad," you are covering that person with clouds instead of the necessary sunlight that would aid in their growth. I also want to include the judgments we place on movie stars, advanced athletes, super heroes, entertainers, etc. These "super-sized" judgments keep them in bondage. There will be a time when they come back to the place of just "being" and they won't know how to handle it. Their lives are all about judgments from other people and how many of you know, there's no such thing as being on the top of the mountain forever. You would miss out on all the wonderful activities at the base of the mountain and the fall from the top can be scary. There is nothing wrong with an opinion that someone is talented and very good at what they do. But like the acorn, you should appreciate the miracle that takes place without glorifying them needlessly. In that way, you can go on to the next miracle, and the next, as if life is set up for that to happen, which it is. But that's just my opinion.

I do understand we live in a world where labels and judgments seem so necessary in order to make choices, however, these labels and judgments should carry a whole lot of love behind your thoughts about them. If you blame, shame or complain, you are operating out of fear. I find the easiest way to love others is to recognize that we are all God's children. If I complain about a certain person, then I am criticizing God's child. If I look at how I would feel if someone criticized one of my kids, I would not be happy with that at all. First of all, that would hurt my feelings and second of all, I would not want to criticize God either, so to speak. Now, does that mean that I go through life never having a disgruntled thought about anyone? Not at all, but I am sure to let go of it a lot faster than I used to. I also know that everything in your life is a reflection of something that might be going on inside of you and it might be a good idea to bring your thoughts back to yourself rather than dwelling on the other person. Why is this happening in my life? What part do I play in this whole scenario? Rest assured if it is in your life it is for your highest good even if it doesn't feel good. It is usually your opportunity for growth. You can apply this method of "Life is a Reflection," by other means such as your car breaking down. If my brakes are not working, it might be reflecting back to me that I have to slow down in my life. Or, if I am having trouble with the alignment, my body might need to be in alignment with some of the dreams and goals I have placed before me. Right now, my car is in the garage with a transmission problem.

It started when I put the key in but I couldn't get it to go forward or backward. It was at a standstill. When I looked at the reflection, I found that my life was at a standstill. I had a goal to write this book, but I found other things to do instead. Now, I am forced to be home and use this time to continue writing. I don't know about you, but I find it highly interesting looking at life through different means. You can also see the reflection of something about yourself through relationships, appliances, finances, and health. All your perceptions are just messages from the Universe. We just need to pay attention.

What about health issues. It has been said that "stress" is the leading cause of sickness. Instead of finding the real cause of pain in our bodies, we take a pill to block out the fact that there are issues to deal with, creating more problems in our bodies, until "dependency" is more important that resolving the real cause of pain. You probably have seen those ads on TV that offer solutions by taking this pill or that pill and then listing the side effects that sound more devastating than the sickness you started with. The sad part is people don't listen and just want what they believe is a "quick fix."

I find it interesting when I read Lousie Hay's book on the mental causes for physical illness and the metaphysical way to overcome them, that they are true to form. Most of the underlying issues come from the lack of love or joy in our lives. When you look at her book, "Heal Your Body," you get an in-depth understanding of how we create the "dis-ease" in our life and how we can change the mental thinking to have a different outcome or reflection of our new thoughts.

By the way, the word "life" also carries the word "if" because your life depends on your choices IF you make conscious and responsible choices to get your desired outcome. How freeing to know that things don't just happen to us…that we really have something to do with every outcome in our lives. To me, that is where the freedom comes in; the freedom to pick and choose what works and what does not. Not everyone is going to agree with your choices, but if you are not a "people pleaser," you will create the life you want a lot faster than most. You have to realize there are basic truths, but there is no ONE WAY to get there. Everyone needs to find their own path and if this book becomes part of your journey…so be it!

Someone else might not agree with it, but that's okay. You don't like the same foods as everyone else, so you don't look to see what someone else is taking first. You help yourself to what you like. You don't get mad at the other person because they are not picking the same foods as you are. How silly would that be? The same thing is true for this book. No ONE person has ALL the answers, but you participate by checking in with yourself and see what might be true for you. This world is way too big to have everyone interested in the same thing at the same time at the same place. That is what makes you a unique individual. There is no "sameness" in life. Similar maybe, but not the same!

LOVE AS a FOUNDATION

When you're feeling low and under duress;
Think thoughts of love to eliminate stress;
With anger and hate there's nothing to gain;
Love and forgiveness will diminish the pain....

Word Whisperer

How many of you know it's important to have a strong foundation? Would you believe that everyone on this planet has the same foundation because we all started with our Creator so we have Source as our base? Even if people don't recognize this truth, they were still birthed into this world to continue a journey of a life time. When you hear we are all one, I believe it is because we all came here connected to the same source in the same way, so we ALL have the same foundation. Now, you can have a foundation and choose not to build on it and it might look different than what someone else has, but the bottom line is we all start with the same foundation which I interpret as love. The separation seems to take place as we grow because we all take on names, titles, different occupations and the foundation seems to disappear as it is now covered with so many different aspects of your life.

When you look at a house, you see the house, not the foundation, so it is understandable that the foundation won't even be given a second thought. Something as important as the foundation is now hidden and all the secondary things become first. We take ourselves so far away from the foundation that our lives become shaky and unfulfilled. Because your foundation, 22 is perfect, whole and complete and you are a part of this foundation, you should be reflecting wellness, prosperity and joy. Sickness, poverty, or any other misalignment is an untruth that you may or may not decide to participate in. This is why it is said "the truth will set you free."

Now, we all start out from the ONE source, which is life itself. It stands to reason "one" can never be divided against itself. You might look at faith and fear as two separate things, but fear is really a misuse of ONE power. You can use this power of Source to operate through you in any way you choose. You can have one pie and slice it and it is an illusion that when you remove one piece from that pie, it becomes separate from the whole pie. But the truth is, that piece is still one with the pie. Take a potato as a foundational truth. You can call it a potato, or French fries, mashed potatoes etc. Now the labels you give it, did not change the fact that it's a potato. It might look different when you mash it or fry it, but the results came from the potato. We all walk around with different labels, titles, and seem to change form from whence we began. We start with a name, then branch off into occupations, such as secretary, doctor, waitress, etc. We slap on these labels which seem to separate us individually. By then, we are so far removed from our foundation of being one with the Source, we cannot even contemplate how that could be.

Now to bring us back to our original form, even before we were born, our parents knew they were going to have a baby. Not baby boy or baby girl…just BABY. Would you all agree we start off the same as a BABY? This is a fundamental truth. The first label we deal with is "boy" or "girl." After that, more labels come throughout the years until we all forget that the baby didn't really change. That beautiful, sweet, innocent, beloved child of God, which is your foundation, has never changed. That is the real truth about you. This is the common ground we all share or are all connected to. Sometimes you have to remove the labels, remove the titles, and remove the negative thoughts about yourself and others to be able to see the true foundation of love. No one in their right mind feels anything but love for a newborn baby. We connect to the truth, even if it is only for a moment, when we connect with that child. Our loving foundation did not change. Just because we took on a name, title, or a number to state how long we have been on Earth, it does not change the foundational truth of love. I might look older now, but I never stepped out of that baby's body to become who I am. Just like the potato, I can slice it, boil it, mash it but it is still the potato I started with. God knew what He was doing when he sent us here as babies with a spirit of love. The baby comes here as a representation of God's love. No judgments, condemnation, guilt, they do not hate you, they aren't even mad at you. They only see with the eyes of God. What I like to do in my classes, is take my audience through a meditation and bring them back to a time when there was only love present. I will present this meditation and when you have quiet time have someone play relaxing music and take you through this meditation process. When you are finished, do the same for the other person. "Meditation" contains the word "mediation" which is a conference between you and your Spirit: If possible, you can have your partner talk you through this process:

Close your eyes and take a deep breath through your nostrils and feel the cleansing air flow into your abdomen as it circulates through your system....Exhale out your mouth, letting go of any tension, or negativity that tries to remain within your body. Take another deep breath and exhale all worries and concerns and bring your attention to a peaceful feeling that is encompassing your body now. Take another deep cleansing breath.....now exhale. I want you to picture in your mind, a small, tiny baby who is content, peaceful, with no worries, who is gazing at you with warm, loving eyes. With your eyes still closed, I want you to look deep into the eyes of this baby who has come to you at this time, to share the love of God with you, without reservation. Feel the love exchange between both of you, the baby who is smiling lovingly at you, so content to be held by you in the comfort of your arms. Without speaking, send thoughts of love to this baby and let this baby know how much you love it and how grateful you are that this baby chose you to go through this experience of unconditional love, with no barriers or labels, just the love connection between you and the baby. Now it's time to name this baby...give it your first name and continue to feel the love that is present within you. Silently call your baby by your name and tell your baby how much you love and appreciate it and how you want to protect and care for this child and let it know he or she is safe within your embrace. Lovingly, hold this baby close to your heart as you become one with this child. Let this baby know, it is a part of you and will always be with you as you place him or her gently into your heart center. You will want to share this baby with others you come in contact with because you are so proud of this goodness that God has blessed you with. Now, your baby is resting peacefully, within your heart, knowing its presence will always be a part of you. Knowing this, you will always want to put the right foods in your body, so that your child receives the proper nutrition it deserves.

You will surround yourself with loving people so that your baby feels the vibration of love at all times. You want only the best for your baby and you will act accordingly to protect and keep your baby safe. Now, when I count to five, you can open your eyes knowing that all is well and you and your child will always be connected. 1...2...3...4....5.

How did that exercise make you feel? Peaceful? Secure? Did you feel the presence of love? Now to take this experience a step further, how you felt about your baby is how your Spirit feels about you. And the only way we move away from that love is by the use of labels, judgments, and thoughts that go against the truth of who we really are. See that loving baby in everyone you meet. You would never intentionally be mean to a baby and everyone carries their own little child within them. That is the God in them. It is your responsibility to address this truth and move away from anything that contradicts the love of God. Storms might come and go but if you stay grounded in truth, you will be victorious. Just remember that in storms, there can be all kinds of dangerous winds, lightning and other things going on, but, what stops the damage that the lightning can produce? It's the fact that your house is "grounded." And now your body that you house your inner child in, can be grounded in truth and love. No amount of damage can consume you if you stay grounded in love. You can lose jobs, people, and things, and still survive and come out victorious.

Like I mentioned before, it's important to remember the child within wants to be fed foods that are nutritious and filled with vitamins. And you wouldn't feed your baby alcohol so why consume it into your body where that child resides. Okay...I hope that explains how you are a part of that baby that never left as you developed into the person you are today. God bless you and your baby within you! No one can take that away from you! Your foundation is strong. "Foundation" has the word "found" in it because you have "found" the real you; the one who started as a precious baby and continued developing into who you are today. Remember, you did not step out of the body of that baby to be who you are. You just transformed into who you are today so in essence, that baby is still as much a part of you as the skin is on your body.

WHAT THE UNIVERSE WANTS YOU TO KNOW

What if race and politics and religion as well;
The wars that are fought and heaven and hell;
Are all made up stories from days gone by;
What if some of your beLIEfs are really a lie....

Word Whisperer

I am looking at the word "Universe" where "uni" represents "one" and if you look closely, the word "serve" is also found in the word "Universe." You have probably heard at least once in your life that "we are all one" on this big planet and we are here to serve. What exactly does that mean? It can be somewhat confusing because we are all individuals which can appear to make us "separate" from others. Yet, it is stated we are all one, even in our illusion of separateness. How can this be?

As I previously mentioned, I believe we are all one because we are all created from the One Source and we are all connected to this Source by an invisible umbilical cord that joins us together as one where that cord meets. Now how many of you know that we deal with the invisible realm every day? Our thoughts are not visible, but we still have them. Faith is not seen until a belief is used to bring the result of faith into the visible. So we do deal with the invisible all the time even if it is not on a conscious level. We cannot see with the visible eye how we are all joined together, but nevertheless, this is so. The way we make this visible is by serving each other in love, forgiveness and compassion. You feel this oneness when you are in the experience of serving or loving one another. When you "gossip" about another person you really "piss" on them so you have to understand the damage that your words produce when they are not in loving form. This really takes practice because we are creatures of expectations and habits which can produce disappointments. We expect someone to act a certain way or we expect something to happen in a certain time frame, etc. This can produce anger, frustration, and an illusion of aloneness.

The Universe wants you to understand that everything is just the way it's supposed to be and to drop the expectations as if you know better than the way it really is. In other words, if something doesn't turn out the way you thought it should, be open to believing it does not have to be a certain way or one way which supports "limited thinking." Just know the "Source" you are forever connected to will gently nudge you in the right direction if you get off track. You are right where you need to be on the way to where you are going. Give yourself permission to relax into the flow, so you are not always swimming "upstream" and tiring yourself out needlessly. This is why we were not sent to this planet one at a time to live out our lives. We are here with the people that came here at this time to help us on our journey. You will never know all the people that touch on your life because you won't be able to see where the ripple effect began. By the same token, you won't be able to see all the people's lives you have touched on by just being who you are and staying in alignment with your Source. Now when I say being in "alignment" with your source, I am talking about God, the Universe, Higher Power, or anything that has the attributes of unconditional love that you want to be a part of in your life.

When I speak of "unconditional love" you might think that you are able to do this easily. But the truth is, "unconditional love' is what is lacking in this world today. You can't love and have wars…You can't love and have punishments…it doesn't match. It just keeps "hate" in place. And nothing changes. You justify your actions and your story sounds good, but nevertheless, it doesn't produce loving results. You might even "label" your actions "righteous" but when the truth supersedes your actions, you are exposed to the truth once again. Love is missing out of your equation. Being "more right" than someone else doesn't qualify you as "better" than anyone else. There's even a fine line with forgiveness. We, as humans, don't really know what it's like to be loved unconditionally in human form. We have no memory of the unconditional love that we were when we first came here as babies. It's no wonder it takes place in the spiritual realm. Our Spirit, which was sent here with us, is connected to the spiritual realm so that we can allow the invisible to manifest into the visible. Our Spirit is the connection to our Source and when we die, our Spirit knows its way home because it never really left. Another important factor that the Universe wants you to know, is to tell the truth, Your stories and justifications do not really matter, If you are the type of person who gets involved in non-committed relationships, it is because you have an issue regarding commitment. Oh yes…water seeks its own level, so whatever you bring into your life is just a reflection of something about you. Funny how we would like it to be about the other person, but again we are going to tell the truth and call it what it is.

I have seen relationships where one person tries to change the other person into what they want them to be instead of picking someone the way they want them to be in the first place. And what about the people who want to have someone else's boyfriend/girlfriend or husband/wife? These are the people who want to be "the one!" It's the old "pick me!"…"pick me!" syndrome. They want to compete with the other person and feel that if they are chosen, that makes them special. But the truth is, it really keeps them at a "fool's level." You are no more special than the other person who is also settling for less than what they deserve. And the truth is, when you want someone else's person, you are not ready for you own. If that person left their partner for you instead, you wouldn't want the relationship, because that person would be less appealing to you when it becomes your own. Furthermore, if you wanted a committed relationship you certainly wouldn't choose someone who cheats in their relationships. Don't think it won't happen to you because you think you are special. If they cheat on one person, they will cheat on another.

And what about those long distant relationships? You think they are appealing because distance makes the heart grow fonder, but the truth is, if you need "long distance" in the relationship, it would never work if the distance was taken out of the relationship. You would just create fights if they were close by to keep "distance" in your relationship. Anyone can deal with the surface relationships from a distance but it's quite another thing to be "involved" and have some depth and meaning to your relationships. This is really how you work out your issues and come out the other side where resolution takes place. Long distance keeps your issues hidden and you don't have to deal with conflict, the bridge that would carry you over to another level of intimacy. Fear keeps you at a distance and you actually try and tell yourself that the relationship is good, but your spirit can not be fooled and doesn't listen to your stories, because lies cannot hide the truth and your spirit is all about truth. You cannot put distance between you and your spirit because it resides within you. Eventually your discomfort will lead you to make necessary changes in your life. The Universe is all about relationships. You are here to have contact with other people that will help you grow. The Universe will support you in your choices because the thoughts you send out there come back to you in the form you requested. But the Universe also knows that truth supersedes lies and it is just a matter of time before your spirit convicts your being as a place where you can no longer fool yourself.

THOUGHTS

There's a fine line between love and hate;
A big distance between have and wait;
The good news is you can have your way;
It starts with a thought and ends with a say...

Word Whisperer

It's no wonder the word "thought" begins with the word "Thou"...which stands for You! Thou art a perfect being. Thou art rich beyond imagination. Thou is really You!!!! It's not that I am trying to twist your tongue, but words have meaning. Just like life has meaning and is for a purpose such as this.

Thoughts are invisible to begin with. Where do thoughts come from? I find it interesting that when babies are born and they are sleeping, they seem to be dreaming a lot of the time. I always wonder how they can dream about anything when they haven't experienced life enough to put anything into thoughts. What could they possibly think about when the knowledge hasn't been taught to them? And what do they know about funny when they crack a smile in their sleep?

Thoughts could be separate entities that come into the mind and transfer messages these thoughts want you to know. You are the vessel and thoughts know where to go because you are like a magnet that calls in these thoughts from the beliefs you chose to accept in this life. Thoughts are a form of energy and need to be experienced through the human soul. Thoughts are attracted to you according to your vibration level. Thoughts are made up of words and words have their own vibration level and can only be expressed through the people they choose. I mean, think about it. And really, that is all you have to do. "Think." That's what makes you who you are...Think has the letter "I" in the middle of the word for a reason. I bring these word thoughts to mind because I want you to understand there is always a deeper meaning to life than just getting out of bed, going to work, and repeating the same pattern over and over again. Even the people at your job have meaning in your life.

It might be someone you don't get along with, but that person is unconsciously teaching you patience, acceptance or understanding, and the situation only changes when you get what you are supposed to get in each circumstance. You might get fired from your job and become angry because you don't realize there is a better job waiting for you somewhere else. You might be the type of person who likes to complain, so you would have to have situations that don't feel right so you can continue this pattern. I actually worked at a "Vision Center" and really did not like the way they operated the business. I knew I was in "vision" because there was something that I needed to see. I got to see the mistreatment of the employees, how the company was all about numbers and sales, and I saw how one of the workers was even "set up" with a camera when she let a friend of hers use her 10% discount card. My title at the job was "Lab Technician" but my pay was that of a teenager starting on their first job. Needless to say, I moved on to my next lesson. The boss I had at the next place was a bully and an egotistical maniac. When things didn't go the way he wanted he would go so far as to throw chairs across the room. I would be intimidated by him and when he would stand in front of me spewing angry words about his business I would agree with him to calm him down. That's right. I would agree with him even if I silently disagreed. You know, one of those people-pleasing mechanisms that kick in every once in a while. My boss loved to be right and really had no respect for anyone who didn't agree with him. How many of you know that people who like to be right, have to have numbers to support their "rightness?" You know, the number of people who agree with them so they can be on top of the world. So I finally got tired of his ranting and raving and when he came over for support in one of his negative commentaries, I simply shook my head and told him "no, I don't agree with you." Well, if he could have fired me on the spot he would have, but he waited a little while to let me go. I think it was around Christmas when I needed the money the most, but I realized it was for my highest good not to go back. I also realized that the lesson for me there was to stand up to the truth and not be intimidated by angry people, but I had to go through the experience to let it go.

I do believe we recreate some of the past that we never handled as children, because my mother could be loud and intimidating at times and I know darn well I told her what she wanted to hear, not necessarily what I really thought. So I finally got a chance as an adult to stand up to what I couldn't resolve in my childhood.

There were other jobs and other lessons and when I wasn't working, I was able to get in touch with my creative side. I realized how much I enjoyed life doing the things I liked and not just the things I had to do. Complaining sometimes feels good because that also gives meaning to your life. You get to survey the happenings in your life and then you decide to go over them again after-the fact. There is an illusion that you get to be right about something and that feels good for a very short time before you create another situation you have to complain about to make yourself feel good. Especially if the person you are complaining to agrees with you and takes your side. Then you get to "puff up" and feel justified in your gossiping mode. Then, God forbid, that person you complained about is nice to you the next day…you get to carry around so much guilt for all the things you said about them you might even make yourself sick or hurt yourself in the process. Is it really worth it to self-destruct and feel bad about your choices when you realize and understand how choices can either lift you up or tear you down. Sometimes you don't look at the "big picture" and say yes to something that turns into a situation that you might want to get out of. On some level you know, but you think you can change the course of the snowball effect, and that does not work.

Nadia Ohar

ABUNDANCE

Whatever you fear the most you create;
If you worry about time, you will be late;
Thinking about money in the form of lack;
Will bring you scarcity and bills that stack....

Word Whisperer

It has been said that there is no such thing as a "money problem." It has to do with your capacity to receive, and of course you have to believe you are worthy and deserving of all good things. Abundance has the word "dance" in it because when you are joyful and free of condemnation, you might want to sing and dance. The word "debt" is very similar to the word "depth" because there is a deep connection to guilt and blame. The more money you owe, the more guilt you carry. There is a reflection of trying to "make up" for something that might have started somewhere in your past. When you owe, you didn't pay enough. In relationships, the pattern plays out co-dependently and consequently you always end up feeling like you didn't give enough, because your giving will never be satisfying, because it is for all the wrong reasons. If you have children, especially if they are grown, you might find yourself trying to fix their problems and again, that is only short term fixes. Just like the charges you put on your credit card…feels good momentarily, but then the bill comes in. Until you make peace with your past, you will remain in debt. You merely have to forgive yourself and understand you did the best you could with what you had to work with. Just because you would do it differently today…that's only because you learned from your lessons and absorbed the knowledge you needed to grow in your experiences. Everyone needs experiences to grow.

It's not in the telling that saves people from doing what they do. Even this book is not to tell you how to live, but to encourage you to lay down the pain that you carry around in your life so you can let in pleasure and enjoyment without paying a price. If you had an opportunity to interview Jesus today, He might tell you that He

35

would have gladly laid down the cross because looking at the world today, no one is spared having to go through their own experiences for the changes needed in their own lives. No one person can make it okay for you. That is something you can do for yourself. You don't have to label yourself with a "negative" tag such as "sinner" because that keeps you in debt. Even if you choose to believe someone died for your sins, you will feel obligated to that someone. You will never get fully into your own life because now you think you owe an outside source, and when you owe, you are in debt. How bad do you have to feel about yourself? Check the balance on your checking and savings account and you will know. It's just a reflection of how you feel about yourself. I would highly recommend you start with the truth that can set you free. You cannot make up for anything you did in the past anymore than you can remove a bruise after the moment it happens. The bruise might fade away eventually but the pain that caused the bruise actually happened. And no amount of kissing the booboo will take away the fact you got hurt. When something happens in your life, you cannot make it "un-happen." You can learn from the experience or you can keep repeating that type of behavior over and over again. Your present is part of your past and you can let go of your past anytime you want. But you might be clinging to your past in order to "fix" the problems you couldn't fix at the time they occurred in your life. Forget it. You can't "fix" the past. You can only decide to start loving yourself enough, the way you are right now, without wishing it had been different for you, and realize you are right where you need to be on the way to where you are going. And so are the other people in your life. You need to stop comparing and competing with others because the truth is "there is no better." It might just be "another way" not a "better way."

Guilt is like a garden…it has to be cultivated to be kept alive. You use guilt to hold you back. If you look closely at the word "guilt" you will see that it contains the letters "tug" hidden in it, because you are constantly pulling yourself back when you start to get ahead. You are constantly creating another debt when you start to pull ahead in your finances. You might even use alcohol to pull yourself back from feeling good because you pay a price with tiredness, hangover, or unclear thinking. When you smoke, you are trying to pull yourself away from life. You know it is harmful but after all, you made mistakes in the past and now it's time to pay the piper. Nonsense!!! You don't owe anyone anything. You only owe it to yourself to stop the lies and experience the truth. Do you really want to get to the place in your life where you enjoy who you are? Don't you want that smile on your face to be real so you can experience healthy living with a full bank account in your name? Stop the lies. You cannot make up for anything in the past, so start with the truth. If there are things you wish you did differently, acknowledge that fact and then add this statement. "I did the best I could with what I knew in the past and now that I have more understanding, I will take that experience as one of my greatest teachers and use it to benefit my life now." You see, nothing that happened in the past is wasted because it was just a bridge to becoming who you are today. I would recommend saying a "forgiveness" affirmation but the truth is, there is really nothing to forgive unless your intention was to consciously hurt yourself or others. And for the most part, if you reacted in anger it was because a part of you was hurting and you wanted to avoid dealing with that pain so you might have lashed out at others. But now that you understand you don't have to respond that way, you will have different results. It's really that simple. We make it hard by hanging on to punishment and blame. Not Necessary!!!

Do not let your past dictate what you are today. Everyone has a past to overcome one way or another. Let your children find their own way. Show them what is possible in life when you let go of the past, because one day they will have to do the same, and they will have to do it without you. Now that you know the real truth about you, continue celebrating the real you! Be open to the abundance that will be pouring into your life because everything the Universe has for you can flow freely now that you are finally ready to receive the good that was always there for you! It is important to remember that when you operate in love, you are already a rich person. Love cannot be measured in terms of finances, but it can be measured in the quality of life. You can lose your money, but love cannot be lost in the heart of the giver. The more you love, the more love you have to give away. And even if you associate "money" with abundance, it is important to remember that money is the "fruit" of your thoughts.

Just like fruit is the result of the tree. Your thoughts can produce more money, but your money can not produce the thoughts you think. The tree produces the fruit, the fruit did not produce the tree. The supply is endless because it doesn't stop at the product itself. Supply is unlimited. That is to dance for!!

THE WHOLE TRUTH SO HELP ME GOD!

Perception can send your whole life reeling;
Without it there would be no reason for feeling;
Your outlook on situations can determine your life;
You can see peace where there appears to be strife....

Word Whisperer

Isn't it interesting that when we are faced with telling the truth ...the whole truth....and nothing but the truth it is followed by the words "so help me God." Why is truth so hard to go by and why do we need the help of God to stay in truth? Is that the Universe's way of telling us that truth is not really as easy as we think it is? I mean a lot of "truth" is defined by the way you see things, not necessarily the way it really is. Is there such a thing as different truths for different people? Or is there really only one truth and each of us has to get to it on different paths? If I wasn't the author of this book, I would love to read on and get another opinion, so I will do the best I can to answer these questions according to my beliefs and not necessarily someone else's truth.

First, I will start with the premise that "untruths" are stated to us as children from grown-up parents that tell us fairy tales that use fictional characters. You can fabricate a story on "fictional characters" and have it turn out the way you want it. But that doesn't always represent life the way it is. It's just a story and stories are not necessarily truth. I mean you can tell the story about little Red Riding Hood and she meets up with the wolf and chats with him, but truthfully, no one is going to stand there and chat with a dangerous animal. This distorts the perception a child might have about dangerous animals. Children are very impressionable and they don't know what is real and what is not. They take your word for it.

Now take the case of Santa Claus, a fat jolly man, dressed in red and is able to fly around the world in a giant sleigh with flying reindeer, and that man who dresses in red will come down your chimney with all kinds of toys for you. This untruth goes on once a year for many years to come. Here are the parents telling lies, but asking that children never tell a lie because after all, your nose could grow just like a certain someone in another fairy tale lie. Then, there's this mouse character that you decide to love because he's so magical and you even go to a place to see him in person, and the truth is he is not really who he appears to be. Oh yeah, he is labeled as someone you know, but who is really lurking behind the costume? And that goes for all the other dress up characters.

Now I am not trying to take the magic out of life, but I am simply trying to show you why it is so hard to know what is real and what is not after being prepped as a kid to follow and believe untruths. Just because there are no signs of devastation when they find out these things are just fantasy doesn't mean there are not repercussions. Everything we do has an effect. If you lie you have the results of a lie even if it's camouflaged into something that seems good. Just like alcohol...you get the high first but there are repercussions from drinking. Okay, so now you know why truth can be a bit confusing right from the beginning. By the way, I just noticed that the word "truth" contains the word "hurt" if you unscramble it. Hmmmmm...more meaning...Now, I am believing that a lot of the lies are told so that someone's feelings won't be hurt. If you are a people pleaser, you will tell someone what you think they want to hear and not necessarily what you believe to be true. It's that way with children with controlling parents. Children want to please their parents so they tell them what they want to hear and also anything that will keep them from getting into trouble. These are patterns developed at a very young age and brought into adulthood and other relationships. Now, the truth has a way of setting you free because truth partners with peace, joy and happiness. Lies partner with guilt, shame and condemnation.

One of the questions I want to ask "Is there only one truth or different truths for different people"? Which brings me to still another question ...What constitutes truth? What is truth made up of? My belief says that truth cannot be changed but beliefs can change all the time. Facts can change. It might be a fact that the forecast says it's supposed to rain and if it doesn't the weather man can change the forecast, but the truth about weather is that it exists in all forms. Sometimes you have to go deeper to see the truth. It might be a fact that you experience sickness, but the truth is it is your Divine Right to be healthy. Even when you see contradictions, it doesn't mean the truth changes.

What I do believe is you can start out with a lie, but the truth always surfaces at some point. This Universe is set up for truth, and anything that covers up the truth is eventually exposed. Darkness cannot remain when light shows up. As my brother Brian once said: "It only takes one candle to light an entire room."

Sometimes the Universe looks like it is divided against itself. You have Republicans and Democrats…you have God and Devil ….Black and White….Love and Hate….Freedom and Fear and so on, but the real truth is there are no opposites. There is one law which I will label truth and anything other than that is just misuse of this one law. That's like electricity is neither good nor bad…it just is, but try misusing it and you will experience some kind of pain. I do believe pain is instrumental in getting us back in alignment with the truth. That's why you have probably heard the saying "It's ALL good!" Sometimes the drama that lies do create can seem exciting and adventurous. But when the dust settles, you are left in a vortex of turmoil that lives on. Once you understand that you create your situations and you are not a victim of life's dislike for you, then you can turn your life around in the direction you want to go. When you take responsibility for your life, you can no longer blame outside circumstances for what happens to you in any given moment. The great thing about this truth is that you can create the life you have always wanted and you don't have to wait for someone else to make it better for you. You are enough.

I often wonder why subjects on life are not taught in school. Students are sent out in the world to wander aimlessly, trying to find their way in a world that doesn't deal directly with history or prepositions and nouns or even some of the math that seemed to encompass such a huge part of their learning time. There is no class on how to communicate in relationships or how to save money for retirement or even how to love one another, that would be helpful in this world today. Sports are a big part of school activities and competition is big because only one team can win. Skills on win-win are not anywhere in sight and rivals are created. Then all this hype ends when you leave school and you are left trying to re-create this energy that seemed like such a big part of your life. The truth is, it cannot be re-created because it's now time for a job and playtime is over. Your gifts and talents are buried as you go out and seek a forty-hour job to survive. Who is really prepared for this type of life? You are born to work more hours than you have for recreation or relaxation. This is what we start to believe. What kind of joy do you get out of a world of hard labor? This is why it is so important to define your gifts and talents at an early age without going through the motions of just going to school to learn what they teach as if you are not the participant of your life, but an agenda of theirs.

Parents, it's also important that you encourage your child every day without putting a lot of importance on grades because the child can lose themselves performing if they think it's all about the grades. Anything outside of them is a reflection, but not a part of who they are. They are not their grades. What happens with that pattern is if your child gets a "C" instead of the "A" they are used to, they can get down on themselves and feel disappointed in their results and start believing there is something wrong with them, instead of realizing a test is something they have to take but it doesn't define who they are. That is hard to do because we do feel a sense of pride when our kids bring home the report cards. I know myself, I have more knowledge now than when I brought my kids up and obviously can't do it all over again, but for some reason, we always find out the answers after-the-fact. But the good news is that books like these are written, and anyone who is supposed to hear this kind of information will have it in their hands in Divine Timing. So once again, everything is just the way it is supposed to be.

Sometimes when you hear "It's supposed to be that way" you can get very confused, because you might lose a loved one prematurely, or you might even know someone who is young and has a terminal illness. I believe that these types of situations are going to affect the people in their lives that need to experience this type of pain for their growth. In other words, there might have been a loss in the past that wasn't dealt with at the time, and now that pain has to be released. The person in your life that is helping you resolve this issue probably contracted a long time ago to come here and help you with this situation, even if it meant leaving this planet, because all spiritual contracts are made in love.

While I am on the subject of looking at situations for our highest good, I want to address a very sensitive and painful topic. I want to address the topic on abortion in a spiritual manner. Anytime a Spirit comes into the Earth's atmosphere, they are already born into this Earth. Even though you can't view this spirit, it still exists. Every Spirit has a purpose to fulfill and when this spirit enters the womb and is forced out by the act of abortion, a higher spiritual event takes place between the mother and this spirit. Most abortions are brought on by fear and the spirit in the womb comes as an adversary to help the mother release an emotion that is lodged in the memory banks of her being. There is a necessary loss that needs to take place in the mother's life that will be instrumental in her spiritual growth. No abortion takes place without a heavy duty impact on the life or lives of others. This planet has a purpose and is designed for beings to experience emotions through situations that are for our highest good. The spirit in the womb has completed the purpose necessary for someone's growth. Death is inevitable whether it's in the womb or out of the womb, but either way purpose can't be avoided. I only write about this delicate topic to raise consciousness to another level. I in no way promote abortion...it's not my call over situations that are destined to take place long before

I had a thought about it. Now this might sound far-fetched to you, but you probably made the same type of deal before you got here and I believe there is someone in your life that needed you here for their growth as well as your own. Isn't it nice to know that everything has a purpose, even if you don't know what it is? It's not in the "knowing" that makes it so...it just is!

IS IT REAL OR IS IT NOT

Each page turned draws you into a plot;
You might find out you're loved a lot;
It's up to you what character you play;
Life has meaning and you have a say.....

Word Whisperer

If you believe something to be true then it's real. The reason I say this is because we live in a Universe where we create our realities according to our beliefs. Our beliefs come from our thoughts about something and our thoughts create or manifest into being. This is why some people cannot understand why we don't all think alike. Someone might think "If it's true for me, then it should be true for someone else also." But the real truth is that not everyone thinks alike. It doesn't make one person more right than the other. It just means we do not all think alike. There would be no reason to have more than one person on this planet if we were all going to think the same. That's why we are all instrumental on this planet at this time because each person is needed to complete the whole puzzle. We signed up for this time because we liked the idea of participating in life in such a way as life is presented at this time. Because everything changes and nothing stays the same, another group of people will participate in life as it is when they manifest on this planet.

Getting back to thinking differently, you would not think it's odd if someone likes chocolate and you prefer vanilla. If you were to have this type of acceptance in all areas of your life, there would be peace and harmony flowing in and out of your life. You could even take that attitude with politics and religion. Instead of coming against someone's beliefs, you would understand it's just their preference and they have a right to be different than you. I don't know if I will see that kind of acceptance in my time here, but I do believe that time will come. The movement right now appears to be raising consciousness and working with thoughts. Like anything else, it is a process that develops over a period of time. This book will speak for itself when it's published and will have a part in changing the world. But right now we do have wars, and we do have an illusion of division even though we are all connected to each other in one way or another. We are actually fighting ourselves and pretending we are not on the same planet. There are bombs being used to destroy this planet and the people who are connected to us and then it's justified that it is a good thing. We buy into thinking if we just kill them the problem will go away. But what is not understood is that the one's doing the killing are part of the problem and until they take responsibility for their part in the fight, the problem will still exist. Funny how it seems to be human nature that we think "it's the other person" and we have little or nothing to do with the fight in the relationship. Blame allows us to remain the same with little or no power over our lives. And we pass this down to our children. They act like we act, and not what we tell them to act like. Then we don't like the way they are acting but we don't raise our consciousness any higher to the point where we see they are acting like we have taught them to act by our behavior.

For instance, you might fight with your spouse in front of your children. Then the kids might fight with each other and you can't understand why they can't get along. Once again, you are in denial about your choices and the repercussions of your actions. Children are blamed for "misbehaving" and are deemed as "bad" or not listening to what you have to say. Oh yes…they hear you alright and maybe you have too much to say and not enough action to back up what you do say. Have you ever encountered the parents who turn around and hit their children because they did not like something they did, and then this child gets in trouble for hitting a kid because they didn't like what he or she did? There are too many double standards in households today.

What about the communication problems in relationships? One person does the telling while the other person has to sit and listen. Especially when it comes to children, some parents are just not interested in what that child has to say. Parents, after all, know best when it comes to their kids. But unfortunately, they are not teaching their children responsibility and they will have to lean on someone else's expertise for the choices in their lives. Confidence cannot be built on someone else's choices. Self-esteem cannot take place when it is someone else who takes the credit for something that child does in his or her life. You know the old glorious statement: "What would you do without me?" Probably a whole lot more if you would just get out of the way!!! Now, I am not trying to be hard on anyone in particular. I have been there many times in my life where I thought I was the hero, and I knew best for everyone else. But what I found to be true is that by sticking my nose in everyone else's business, my life went by the wayside. Then I looked around for someone else to make it better for me. And how many of you know that someone else cannot fix your problems? That's why they are called "YOUR" problems. So now, I am finally grateful to be in the life that God blessed me with and I have stopped wishing I was someone else and finally made peace with myself and my surroundings. Now that I have claimed my life, I can't wait to see what the Universe has in store for me. I am ready to claim my good and can't wait to give back with the overflow coming my way!

Nadia Ohar

MATTER MATTERS

If there's no love the music will die;
Flowers will droop and birds won't fly;
Oceans dry up and babies won't grow'
Isn't it better to Love now that you know...?

Word Whisperer

Ok, it's my responsibility to make sure this book is anything but boring. I find life is so much more than just a routine you do every day. When I stop to think about life and how everything matters, I also realize that everything is made of matter. Matter of fact, I looked up the definition of "matter" and the dictionary says "that which occupies space and is perceptible by the senses; substance." I'd have to say that everything we bring into this world from the invisible into the visible matters. Our thoughts are invisible, but we get to see them manifested into form. What if these thoughts were invisible entities like we once were and they look to be born into this world like we once were. Just like single letters need other letters to make a word, these thoughts need us to live. I bet you didn't realize, you are to thoughts, as the body is to Spirit. Everything needs a vehicle to move forward into destination. When the vehicle is no longer available, thoughts will live on and never die, just as we continue on after our vehicle expires. We go back into the invisible where we were before, possibly waiting to be born again or help others from the other side where it still matters. There is also faith that is invisible and brought into this realm by your thoughts. It is comforting to know that thoughts are chosen and not just something that happens to you. If you don't like your life, change your thoughts about your life and you will see life change for you. It's really that simple. I wish it was mandatory to record all conversation during the day and then mandatory to listen to the replay at the end of the day. Then see how many times you say negative statements like "I can't"…"I don't have enough time"….."He doesn't like me"….."I wish I had something better"…."You don't understand"……blah blah blah….really. Why not turn your life around by using different affirmations that really matter. "I can…I will find a way….I will make time to do that….what you think about me is none of my business… I am grateful for what I do have…"and you can make your own list. You know what you need and you know you can have it by starting with your thoughts that matter.

Speaking about what matters, I want to share something about my life that brought me to this place where I am right now in my life. Looking back, I would have to say I was always somewhat of an adventurer. Nothing for me was going to be the norm and little did I know that pattern started even before I lost my mother at the age of twelve. I remember as a child, I was always interested in experimenting with chemistry sets to see what changes would take place by mixing this and putting that together. I had a neighborhood kid that lived close by and we took a jar and started with water as a base. Then we added grass, toothpaste, ink, shampoo, and all kinds of various substances to see if something would change.

Well, I walked away shaking my head, knowing that there just had to be one more ingredient that would have made the difference because nothing changed in that jar. Change did come into my life but it wasn't from a jar of ingredients. .

It was a bright sunny day, and my Father, three brothers, my sister and I were at home sitting in the living room. My Mother suddenly started going into convulsions out of nowhere. One minute she seemed okay and the next minute she was struggling to breathe. My father held her in his arms and I ran out the door to get help at the fire dept. on the corner, but didn't quite make it there because my older brother ran past me to get there first. I was so relieved he got there first because I wasn't quite sure how I would tell these men that my mother seemed to be dying out of the clear blue. Everything after that seemed like a dream.

I stayed outside on a neighbor's porch while they removed my mother from the house. My sister and I were transported to my Aunt and Uncles and my brothers went to another relative's house while we waited for the news. I remember playing the song "Tragedy" by the Fleetwoods over and over again. When the phone rang I could tell by the horrified look on my Aunt's face that she got bad news. She didn't give me the news right away but I knew by the look on her face. Later that night, my sister and I went home and my aunt, who was my mother's sister, was waiting there to give us the news of my mother's passing. I remember her calling me into the room to tell me what I already knew, but, I walked out of the room because I felt like if I didn't hear the news then it meant it didn't happen. But eventually I had to go back in and hear that my mom had died. I can't explain how it felt as a child to look outside at the big world and know that you were never going to see your mother ever again. I walked around that night saying the name "Mom" over and over, because as a child I knew I would never be able to use that name again and I was afraid I would forget it. A week later I was back in school like nothing had ever happened. I had to fit into a world where life went on but nothing felt real to me. I played along like nothing had ever happened to me and felt guilty when I would laugh or start to have a good time because deep down I knew I wasn't matching my reality. I had trouble focusing on anything in school because nothing really mattered that much because after all, you could leave this earth at any time. Besides, I was now different from everyone else who had their mom and I didn't want to be reminded of my loss or the fact that I was now different from others.

Then we got the news we had to move out of our home and move in with my Grandmother who was not my idea of a loving grandmother. And she proved me right. She never resolved any of her childhood issues and brought them into the present. She had raised her brothers, raised her four sons and now she was raising five other children. She didn't like girls and that didn't help my sister or me trying to adjust into a new life. My father worked full time and would come home and listen to complaints from her about how bad we were and how we didn't do anything right and my father would pop open a beer can and let her rant for twenty minutes. Then the TV would go on and he would lose himself in Lawrence Welk or some other show he liked before he would end up falling asleep. This went on for years with no resolution. I got myself involved with my first real love and was engaged by the time I was sixteen or seventeen. We used to go out drinking and partying every weekend and then one day out of the blue I told him I didn't want to be engaged anymore and gave him back the ring. He was beside himself. Looking back, I feel bad because he was really someone I thought I loved more than anything, but I was never going to marry him because I was never going to take anything all the way. I just wanted the freedom to come and go as I pleased and didn't want to commit to anyone or anything. Maybe for a short time, long term was out of the question. It was such an illusion that I could live a normal life but it was always short lived.

Then I got engaged again for a short time before I pawned the ring to have something nice to wear so I could go out and party again. My fiancé had left to go to England where he went to see his mother and when he got back I had already started dating someone else. I told him I lost the engagement ring when I went swimming at the beach and I avoided seeing or talking to him after that. Then I met my husband-to-be at one of the clubs and we started going out. He was in the Navy and by then I was 21 and it was time to think about getting married. Our relationship was not stable and was shaky right from the start. I came from a place where I didn't trust anyone and it was going to be no different with him. I eventually got pregnant so I could seal the deal, subconsciously, and have him marry me so we could start a family. What I didn't know then is we never resolved the issues that were with us before marriage, so there was no way we were going to make it once we were married. I was insecure, immature, and never really grieved the loss of my mother. My husband had a tough childhood and left home when he was young to join the Navy and get out on his own. Neither one of us were nurtured properly so we had to use our relationship to face the problems we both carried within ourselves. Our marriage was built on "right" and "wrong" issues. We tore each other down and we never built each other up so our marriage could last. The drinking continued and fighting persisted. I delivered a baby girl seventeen days after we were married. There was no honeymoon and no wedding bells ringing. I came home after we were pronounced man and wife and never felt so alone. We stayed together for awhile and in between fights, we would make up and find time to conceive another baby girl eighteen months after the first one. It helped take the focus off of our dysfunctional home, and two years later came another baby girl. When I look back on our marriage, I can understand why I thought, by getting married, this would have to last forever. We bought a house, had three girls, and it just seemed that was how you were supposed to live. Fighting was still the theme in the household and we were both co-dependent. I was starting to read self-help books on codependency and realized that I never felt like I had the right to be happy. If I had something to say, my husband demeaned it, because he had to be the smart one and I was supposed to be the one who needed him. It was never going to be a two-way street. I would have to keep myself "down" to make him happy.

When my baby daughter was five years old, I decided to go with my sister and get a job. I still didn't feel confident enough to go on my own. My husband had left for Spain where his job had sent him. My sister and I ended up at a dog track and got hired that night. It's no accident that I got hired at a place where there was gambling, drinking, and all kinds of dysfunction. When I say you draw in the issues from who you think you are, I had the results of my thoughts.

It didn't take long for my marriage to take a turn for the worse. While I was out working, I had men thinking I was the greatest thing since ice tea…..and since I needed my ego stroked, I felt that everyone on the outside loved me more than my husband did. My husband would go out drinking and dancing with other women and consequently we kept getting further and further apart. We went to marriage counseling, marriage encounter, Life Spring trainings, and nothing could save our marriage. We were too busy blaming each other to ever have it any different.

I moved out with the three girls and found an apartment to live in. Life never got any easier and I found myself moving from place to place, living with my sister-in-law and her children and then moving in with my sister and her family until I could get on my feet. Life was not easy and I knew nothing of positive living or creating new experiences for myself. I started dating one of the bartenders at work and thought he was the one for me. I didn't recognize at that time, "water seeks its own level." I was not divorced when I started dating him and he obviously had commitment issues too or he wouldn't have started dating me. When I became free and could be in a committed relationship with him, he bailed. No surprise, because I started studying "the law of attraction" before all these situations took place. Then to ease my pain, I got involved with another non-committed person and got pregnant. By now my girls were teen-agers and it was like starting all over again. But this time

I decided to do it differently. I said no to living with this man who had a drug and drinking problem. I was going to give my son my last name and raise him myself. As it turned out, I did just that. His father was involved very little, but I finally accepted that I had to turn my life around and stop being angry at the way things were. I always felt like a victim and never realized my choices were holding me back and that things weren't just happening to me.

I eventually left the dog track, took a computer class and worked in a doctor's office. Slowly, but surely, I was improving my life. I read self-help books, used affirmations, stopped going out to the bars and little by little I started taking my life back. I think this is why this book is so meaningful to me, because if I can help one person to know they are not alone, and that there are people out there who want to encourage and support you in your growth. You need to know that the Universe is here for you to enjoy your life. It doesn't have to be a struggle. I know this is true because you matter!!!!!

PRAY FOR ACCEPTANCE & THE LOVE WILL FOLLOW

When you say hello and give away smiles
The ripple effect can go on for miles;
The effort it takes is really not hard;
You can even start from your back yard....

Word Whisperer

When I look back on my life, I realize most of my unhappiness was caused by wanting someone or something to be different. First I had to judge the situation in a negative way before I could come to that conclusion. I would find a reason not to like something and then complain about it. I could find fault with just about anything and for some reason that made me the Queen of "being right." How many of you know how it feels to be right about something? You know, that surge of power you feel….that sense of righteousness and "better-than-thou" feeling. What I finally came to realize is that type of power can make you feel good for awhile, but you have no one to share that happiness with because "being right" causes isolation. You are set apart from everyone because after all, you know best! You sit alone at the top of your judgmental righteousness not quite sure why your happiness starts to dwindle and you might look for another situation to complain about.

I know, for me, when I was done making judgmental statements, I would start feeling guilty, but that complaining felt so good in the beginning. It was like watching a soap opera where nothing is really working out for the characters, but having the strong desire to keep watching the show again, knowing full well something was always going to be wrong, either in relationships or deceptive lies. Looking back, I have to say, I did come from a family of right and wrong. There were no "in betweens." I took that pattern into my marriage and my children were taught that same negative pattern. I wasn't able to teach proper communication skills, so consequently I had to live through their relationships where I heard the same right and wrong issues surface when they talked to each other. And the thing about "right" and "wrong" is that no one can see the other person's viewpoint as valid. There's no room for a two way conversation and people are talked "AT" rather than "WITH." I have seen that type of situation in my own family with two of my daughters fighting with each other, using words that tore each other down. Consequently, they ended up not speaking to each other and it hurt me to see the results of my "right" and "wrong" thinking that I poured into them. At first, each one of them refused to see their part in this destructive behavior and took no responsibility for the hurt they caused each other in their relationship.

There's also the issue of "perfection" that is brought into these types of relationships. Something has to be a certain way in order for it to be okay. There is very little time to enjoy life and most of the time is spent feeling "stressed" which is attached to every outcome. The good news in all of this is that I learned a very valuable lesson. I vowed I would be conscious of every word that came out of my mouth and I would no longer criticize, judge or condemn another person. I know with the help of God, I can do this. The reason I say "with the help of God" is because my experience of God has always been from the place of love. I have never had a bad thought about God and I know enough not to fight with Him. Not out of fear...but out of common sense. I will say that when I feel the need for forgiveness, I turn to God and know in my heart that I am forgiven. And it's not that I believe God has to forgive me because He probably hasn't judged me anyway, but it's my way of letting go of any guilt I might carry for my actions. I can then start with a clean slate and feel refreshed about my life. I am starting to realize that the judgments about others were just allowing me to keep the wall in place, the invisible wall I had built around my heart, to keep pain out. What I didn't realize was the wall was really keeping the pain locked in. So now, at this time in my life, I am willing to let the wall down and really let people in and understand that being hurt is a choice. I can look at situations in a negative way, or I can look at something and see it for what it is. Not a plot to hurt me, but just people being people. And by the way, by taking the wall down, I am also allowing abundance to enter into my life. I am done blocking good things coming my way. I still love quoting my brother Brian when he said, "It is better to light one candle than to curse the darkness." I prefer to be that light which causes darkness to fade. The feeling of love is far greater than the temporary sense of power I used to get from judging others and trying to be right and gain my self-worth by putting others down. By the way, my two daughters are no longer fighting with each other and they resolved their issue in a calm and loving manner. I am so grateful when I see the results of living in love. I am so proud of my children!!! Thank you God for wisdom, but most of all thank you for your love!!!!

Nadia Ohar

DIVINE HEALTH

If you want to find something wrong you will;
When you feel bad you reach for your pill;
What if your life is just music, a song;
The rhythm you choose is where you belong...

Word Whisperer

I believe we create most of our health issues through our thought processes. Most of these issues are created by holding on to resentment, unforgiveness, past regrets and bitterness. Fear is the key factor in most of these issues. Each part of the body has a way of letting you know when there is an issue that needs to be addressed, confronted, and released. Pain is a key reminder for those who tend to neglect or ignore a certain reality that needs to be brought to the light for healing.

Knowing that it is a possibility that some of your mental patterns can create sickness or disease in your body, are you willing to change some of your thought patterns? Start with the thought that it is your Divine Right to be healthy. Claim that as your right now!!! For others who are dealing with chronic pain, first identify what part of your body is holding that pain and understand there are underlying messages being sent your way. If your neck is in pain you might have issues around being right in your life. If you have back pain, you might not feel supported by life, itself. Legs move you forward in life, so any problems with feet or your legs could be resistance to moving ahead in your life.

And even when sickness is labeled diabetes, you might be lacking love and also see life as hard and "unsweetened." Cancer can be caused by resentment, bitterness, and holding on to pain of the past. Whatever you are dealing with, just know that you are in charge of your body...not your body taking charge over you! It's like being the captain of a boat....you don't let the boat lead...you take the wheel!!!

The nice thing about this life is there are so many ways to choose how you bless your body with different therapies that appeal to your senses. You can use affirmative prayer and affirm the truth about you, which is the fact you are one with God and there is no sickness in Spirit and you are a Spiritual Being. Some people like to use sound vibrations to tune the cells, tissues, and organs of their bodies. Your body is like an instrument and sometimes it has to be fine-tuned. Sound is energy that can be transmitted as sound. Sound travels in waves through the air and is measured in frequencies. Frequency refers to pitch, the high and low quality of sound. The higher the pitch, the faster the vibration will be. You can experiment with sound and see what resonates with you. Fast music heightens your energy level, but pay close attention to some of the words in songs that might be vibrating at a low level. Words carry frequencies that will affect your mood, which in turn affects your body. Bring soft music into your relaxation time and see how your body responds to different types of music. There is also "color therapy" which uses color as a healing tool. Color vibrates at a specific, individual frequency as do the glands and organs of the body. The eyes convert light into a kind of energy which travels through your nervous system, which can affect all body functions. Studies have shown that when color is introduced to the human system, it causes cellular and hormonal changes thus bringing cells into balance with color.

I only mentioned a few but I am sure there are so many other ways to get in touch with your own needs. I believe resolution of conflict or other issues exposed will result in a reflection of your natural state of Divine Health. Love and faith in the goodness of life will also promote healthy living. You can also meditate and participate in different types of yoga to promote a sound mind and body. We live in an unlimited Universe and not everyone chooses the same way to heal. There is an abundance of holistic measures as well as the use of conventional doctors. I only mentioned a few, but I am sure there are so many other ways to get in touch with your own needs.

HEALTHY FOOD CHOICES

You are the vehicle that gets you around;
Check your engine and see how you sound;
The fuel that you use is the food that you take;
Your words will determine the miles you make...

Word Whisperer

I want to make sure I do a chapter on healthy eating habits because when we deal with "Mind," "Body," and "Soul," I believe the food we eat has a lot to do with the body. I have talked a lot about the "mind" and "thoughts" and now it's time to give you some healthy choices when it comes to food. I don't know about you, but I have always been fascinated by the colors of the rainbow or the rainbow itself. There have been many meanings people have associated when it comes to the rainbow. One meaning is the covenant that God gave to His people; another meaning is the pot of gold at the end of a rainbow and maybe just the beauty of the colors in the sky after the storm. For me, I use the colors of the rainbow in some of my work and also when I make my inspirational bracelets. I have one bracelet that sparkles the colors of the rainbow with an inspirational message which reads:

Sometimes in life, you weather a storm:
After the chaos, a rainbow will form;
Hard times may come, but not to stay;
Wear this bracelet; be blessed today!

There's something about color that lifts your spirit. It's that way when we choose the clothes we wear, or paint the walls in our homes. Color enhances moods and is used today in color therapy. Even the foods we eat are colorful. Red is the color of passion and most red foods contain Vitamin C. Some of the foods in the red food category are apples, raspberries, cranberries, strawberries, red cherries, red grapes, pomegranates, plums, rhubarb, watermelon, tomatoes, red peppers, radishes and red onions, just to name a few.

The yellow and orange foods which have beta carotene converts to Vitamin A which is important for healing the gastrointestinal tract, lungs, and skin. Beta carotene provides antioxidant protection against substance that can damage cells. One cup of cooked pumpkin contains a huge percent of the daily recommended intake of beta carotene. This protects cholesterol from oxidation, which in turn assists in the prevention of heart disease. Beta Carotene is a powerful antioxidant and anti-inflammatory nutrient. Anti- oxidants have the power to protect you from cardiovascular disease, wrinkles and cancer. Here are some of the recommended foods in this category: apricots, papaya, oranges, carrots, pineapple, mangos, pumpkin, squash, cantaloupe, nectarines, peaches, and sweet potatoes.

Moving on to the green foods where Vitamin B is prevalent among the dark green leafy and cruciferous vegetables and are the most potent cancer preventing foods you can possibly eat. When you choose a watercress salad, you are healing every cell, and boosting every organ system in your body. To ensure a long and healthy life, eat more spinach, mustard greens, broccoli, kale, cucumber, green beans, asparagus, avocado, spinach, lettuce, Brussels sprouts and zucchini.

Now it's time to talk about the blue and purple foods. The darker the food is, the higher the antioxidant levels are. The purple pigment in fruits and vegetables contain flavonoids including resveratrol, which can help decrease blood pressure. Purple foods are also ulcer fighters. Eggplant, black berries, blueberries, figs, purple cabbage, cherries, grapes, and beets are just some of the dark foods to choose from. These are just some of the colorful foods but there are plenty more to choose from.

Vitamin D foods are often white such as milk, mushrooms and fish. Vitamin E foods are brown such as wheat germ, almonds, and sunflower seeds. While we are on the subject of healthy eating habits, Deuteronomy 8 in the bible shows where the Israelites are promised "a good land…, a land of wheat and barley, of vines, figs, and pomegranates, a land of olive trees and honey." Wheat can be found in everything from bread to pasta and cakes. Whole wheat products if they are 100% whole wheat, contain 30 percent of your recommended daily fiber intake, and high levels of manganese and magnesium. Wheat is thought to increase your energy level and lower your risk of type II diabetes, gallstones and other health issues. Barley can be found in breads and cereals and also in hearty soups. Because it is high in fiber, barley is good for intestinal health and can lower cholesterol and reduce your risk of colon cancer and type II diabetes. It can also reduce the symptoms of arthritis. Grapes contain nutritional compounds called flavonoids which are believed to reduce your risk of blood clots and protect your body from bad cholesterol. Rich in antioxidants, grapes may provide protection against cardiovascular disease, particularly in women. Figs are sweet fruits, and can be eaten dried or fresh and are high in potassium which can help control blood pressure. They are a fruit source of calcium which can help preserve bone density. Pomegranate are strange looking seed fruits and can be taken in juice form. The fruits are rich in antioxidants which help prevent blood clots by keeping blood platelets from clumping together. Pomegranates may also help reduce the risk of breast cancer and lessen the symptoms of arthritis. Olive oil contains antioxidants that are thought to protect against the oxidation of LDL cholesterol compounds. They are also high in monounsaturated fatty acids, which are called the healing fats because they lower the effects of bad cholesterol while raising good cholesterol levels. High in Vitamin E, olive oil is thought to prevent colon cancer and it helpful in fighting gastritis and other stomach ailments. Raw honey, in addition to being a natural sweetener, is filled with antioxidants.

There is enough variety in each category, that I am sure you will find something healthy you would enjoy eating. I don't want to leave out drinking plenty of water each day so you replenish your body. We are 70% water and the Earth is 70% water and we can heal ourselves by consciously expressing love and good will. Water has the ability to receive a wide range of frequencies. Think of words in terms of vibration. If I write the word "love" it carries a vibration and water can be imprinted with that same vibration. Dr. Masaru Emoto found that water exposed to words of love showed brilliant, complex and colorful snowflake patterns when frozen as opposed to water that did not have loving input. Music, visual images, words written on paper, and photographs have an impact on crystal structure. I, myself, treat water with words, light, and music so that when I take a drink, my body can experience the healing qualities needed to restore balance and wellness in my system. Again, we are only limited with our thinking and how far we let our thoughts take us. I, for one refuse to have limited thinking and I am sure I will learn even more techniques and tools that will help to improve my quality of living. I will say that I do start my day being grateful for everything that is in my life and when something happens, such as my car breaks down, or my cell phone doesn't work, or whatever the case may be, I do understand that it all happens for a reason even if I am not aware of what those reasons are. That takes the "sting" out of the situation and brings me back to reality. I like to incorporate the saying "It's all good!" so when I am confronted with any problem that shows up, I can deal with it without the stress I would probably feel if I didn't know better.

Speaking of stress, I haven't decided what I would name this book once it is birthed through me. I haven't given it a "gender" but I really should give it a name. I was leaning towards "What do YOU think?" because it is directed at raising your consciousness and supporting good thoughts into being and obviously what you think matters. I also like "What you think matters" because I believe thoughts turn into "matter" and they really do matter also. I like meaningful phrases that you might have to stop and think for a moment and ask yourself "what is she really saying?" You will know the title as soon as this book is published. It might not be any of the two tittles I just mentioned, but time will tell. In the meantime I have pages to fill and I really want something different for you to read that will contain some "aha" moments. I think I will consult the Universe and ask if there is anything special that I should write about. I will see what floods my consciousness and continue sharing with you. I have always heard the phrase, "Ask and you shall receive."

LIFE IS A REFLECTION

Life is a canvas and you are the paint;
You can be bold or you can be faint;
The new day is your paint brush to use;
Color your world any way you choose;

Word Whisperer

How nice to be able to see the whole picture when it comes to your life. I mean, all you have to do is look at the car you drive or see the place where you live and this says a little something about you or what you think you deserve. Material items don't define who you are, but sometimes when you don't have the things you say are important to you, it might say you are afraid to have them. Worse yet, it might be a reflection of not loving yourself enough to think you are worth having what you say you want. I know for me, I have started observing the way my life is by the reflection around me. Right now, I am without a car and I realize I never saved for one even though my car was older. That is typical of the way I run my life. I handle situations as they arise but I never prepare for the future. I just believe that things will take care of themselves and quite frankly, I used to have dependency issues, so if something went wrong I would have a backup or someone would come to my rescue. But this time it's different. I am the one who has to come to my own rescue so I can let go of depending on someone else to fix the problem and I can stop being a victim. I am going to have to create a way to increase my income so that I can live a fulfilling life and be an example for my children so that they see that an abundant life is possible. I trust God/Universe to open doors for me and to keep me on the path I need to be on. I do this by meditating and asking God questions such as "What do I need to do to turn my life around?" I usually get an inner knowingness more so than a voice telling me what to do. I believe the answers are always there, but by asking, it means you are ready for answers.

Sometimes you have to let people into your life that are willing to help and support you through hard times, but there is a fine line between having help from someone else and not doing what it takes to eliminate the need for help. In other words, when I am without a car, I am truly grateful when I need a ride to the store and I can rely on someone to take me there. However, I don't expect people to give me a ride around the block just to have something to do, or drop me off at the movie house and pick me up later. In other words, I don't take advantage of other people's kindness. My children have always been wonderful in helping me out, but this time I want to be an example and handle what I need to handle to get ahead in my life. If someone else is constantly doing it for you, you cannot feel good about getting through situations that come into your life because you are used to everyone doing it for you. That only reinforces the "loser: in you, rather than being someone who had to go through circumstances that were a little difficult and came out victorious. That's how we build confidence and self-esteem in our lives. Someone said "no pain…no gain" and they could be right. Anyway, I personally don't want to go through life with everyone feeling sorry for me. There's nothing to get excited about when you walk around with a "poor me" attitude. How about a thought "I can do all things through Christ who strengthens me" or what about that little train that had to keep reminding himself "I can! "I can!" and he did! Yes, it takes practice…especially if you feel defeated at the starting line. But that doesn't mean you stay there. If you want to run the race, then you keep going to the finish line no matter how long it takes you to get there. It doesn't really matter if you are first, second or third and so on…the victory really comes from finishing the race. Especially because you now have a mindset that lets you know you are doing the best you can at any given moment, subject to change when the time is right.

Our biggest enemy is comparison. We watch to see how someone else is doing and then we decide if we are good enough in comparison to the way they are.

That is a no-no!!!! I can tell you I have, at one time or another, participated in that energy, and I can also tell you, it was very destructive. Not only does that type of pattern cause you to have ill feelings against the person you think is better than you, but you are really judging yourself not good enough and that is exactly what your life will reflect back to you. The broken car, the small apartment, the empty wallet…yes, all a reflection of something you put into your consciousness and re-enforced that you were not good enough. Liars don't have rewards…they have punishments. And that is exactly what you do to yourself every time you tell yourself you are not good enough. Do not look at someone's life and wish it could be yours. You don't know what they had to walk through to get to that place. Send them love because you cannot hold two thoughts in mind at the same time. So if you find yourself envious, jealous, or angry, about someone else…just breath deep and bring in the truth that there is no "better," only "what is" or "just another way." All thoughts of measurement and standards are made up from individual people that decide how high the bar should be set. Again, it's only individuals with their own thoughts…not something the world should take on as a set-in-stone standard of living. You have to find your own way and if you do it in love, then you go higher than any visible marker that others set in place. If you come from love, you don't have to set anything in stone…everything falls into place and your life will reflect happiness, peace and joy.

How many people work their lives away and wait until they retire to think they will enjoy life now…Most times it doesn't happen because by the time you retire you already have a set pattern of working hard and you can't relax by not working. I used to think that the people in jails had it better than I did because I would work a nine-to- five job being confined in a building, buying my own meals, and then being "let out" at night to go home and then come back the next day and start again. I used to think that the people in jail at least got meals served to them and maybe some kind of recreation. Anyway, I had no business comparing what others had or didn't have. It was really up to me to decide how I wanted to live. I stayed at a job for five long years before I finally left to work part- time somewhere else so I could have more time to use and enjoy my writing skills. I didn't make my life about money, even though I had my struggles, but I did have what I needed and I was grateful for that. When I wasn't busy working for others I found out more about myself and my creative abilities. I found that I loved writing tributes for people for different occasions and that poetry came very easy to me. I felt a "spiritual connection" in all my writings and I started using my talents more and more. I was always interested in "holistic healing" and wrote my own affirmations according to the needs in my life and shared them with others. I enjoyed encouraging and uplifting anyone that crossed my path that needed to hear the "good news" about life. I created a "Spiritual Path Adventure" by using my writing skills and the messages that came to me from the Universe. This adventure allowed people to come and walk their path after they chose at least 20 of the message cards that I made and put them down in front of them to walk their path. Then numbers are drawn one at a time and a person would walk that many spaces and turn over the message they landed on. I was amazed as personal messages unfolded every step they took on their Path. Angel Card Readings were also an avenue for me to tap into the spiritual part of life and help others who needed to hear more uplifting messages from the spiritual realm. I went on to publish my first book titled, "A Passage Through 9/11," available on Amazon.com, which dealt with the pain of loss and the healing energy of love. I can honestly say that writing is a passion of mine, as well as talking with people who share the same spiritual connection as I do. It is always a joy and a privilege to help others, because in the process I am really helping myself and I do believe we all have the answers within us, so the mentor just unlocks what you already know. Even this book will fall into the hands of anyone that needs to hear the words that will make a difference in their lives. I am grateful that I can be used as a channel for the Universe to connect with the lives of others. God created me with everything I need to do just that. I used to wonder what the difference was between the Universe and God, but what I have come to understand is that God is individualized as the Universe just as we are all individualized as beings of this same God, which makes us all one because it all starts with God and continues as God in different ways. If it's easier to understand "energy" than it might be easier to picture the term "electricity" that is individualized through appliances, computers, televisions, etc. …different forms, same electricity. God is like the power source we connect to in order to function properly. Misuse of Universal laws can result in harmful results just as electricity can result in fire and shock if misused.

ADDICTIONS

c"HANGe is when you "hang" up the old and put on the new;
It's important to be involved in something that's good for you;
One day you will realize the obstacles you had to overcome;
Were just the stepping stones needed to help you become.....

Word Whisperer

Notice the word "Add" at the beginning of the word "addiction." You are adding or taking on something you don't need to have. If you look closely you will see that the letters "c," "o" and "n" are in that word which is exactly what you do to yourself. You con yourself into thinking the addiction you take on isn't really harming you because you experience the instant gratification before you experience the after effects. When you first choose to smoke, drink, or take other drugs into your body, you are actually pretending that something is good for you. You pretend that booze relaxes you, or smoking calms you down, when in fact you could do that for yourself if you just used the right thoughts to get you through the rough spots in your life.

I remember when I used to drink alcohol, I conned myself into believing that alcohol was my friend. I was so used to unavailability in my life that I actually liked the idea I could have the bottle anytime I wanted because it was available whenever I wanted it. I also liked the idea it made me feel good plus I was the one in control, and I would be the one to decide when I would let it in and when I would release it. Such stories you tell yourself to fool the consciousness into believing that something is good for you so you don't have to give it up. And then the day comes when you realize you can't give it up because now the body craves this destructive substance and your cravings have charge over your life.

You gave up control a long time ago when you first decided to harm yourself. If you cared enough about yourself, you would never have started this destructive behavior to begin with. Somewhere along the line you gave up your control and allowed someone or something in your life to tell you what was best for you and you carried that pattern into the arms of addiction. You believed an outside source rather than your own ability to judge and know best when it came to knowing the truth about who you were. You may have been in an abusive relationship because you didn't think you deserved to be loved and then you fed your addictions to prove that you weren't worth loving. Another story! The truth is every time you lit that cigarette, every time you put that drink to your mouth, or indulged in other destructive patterns, you were just re-living the pain of the past and you kept feeding that hurt so it stayed alive. The pain surfaces, you medicate and actually feed that pain, and it sticks around till the next time. If you stopped doing what you do, the pain would surface and then you would have to take charge and confront the pain and then stand up to it because it isn't going to leave until you tell it to. You have to take back the reins in your life and stand up to whatever the old issues are that keep on surfacing. You would be surprised just how good you would feel naturally, when you achieve that goal of not smoking or drinking or refusing to take pills or any other drugs and just ride out the waves of depression or tears that surface when you don't push your feelings back down again. Your cigarette is NOT your friend. That drink can't love you back! The porn can't satisfy any real need! The pills can't permanently ease your pain and are filled with side effects! Once you get a grip on reality you will be able to stand up to anything that doesn't fit into who you really are as a Divine Being. Your Divine Nature is just waiting for you to claim who you really are and celebrate the wonderful you! When you understand that part of you that never changes, that never leaves, that will be with you till the day you die, you will then be able to connect to the part of you that is perfect, whole and complete. You will never look on the outside for something to complete you ever again! Not food, not alcohol and not even other people who you think might complete you.

COULD THIS BE YOU?

When you can hear without sound and can see without sight;
When you think something's wrong and you know that it's right;
These are the moments that whisper "Just Be who you are"
Remember, You are the one that has brought you this far...

Word Whisperer

I asked the Universe for a profound message that someone could relate to and I wanted to share something that would make a difference in this person's life. There is someone literally fighting for their life and the Universe wants this person to know that life is not something to give up, but to hold tight because there are changes just around the corner that you don't even know about. These changes are coming to you in a fast manner and you will be surrounded by love that you never experienced before. You will be able to help others because you are going to pull yourself out of the pit you are in right now and make that decision to clean yourself up because life is worth living. The pain you are feeling is just temporary and needs releasing. So allow the tears to flow and wrap your arms around your body and know that you are enough and that you do matter just for the fact that you were born, When and where you were born and everything that took place up until now has been necessary to bring you to this place where you will choose life and not death. Just know you are not alone and just because most of your support comes from the invisible, doesn't mean it won't manifest into being just as long as you trust there is more to life than what you have experienced up to now. I am going to ask all the readers to close their eyes and send you love because you deserve to know how life is really supposed to be lived. You have people you don't even know sending love your way right now, because you matter!!!! This invisible energy is truly going to help you get on your feet and when you do, you have to pay it forward. There is someone just like you who needs a hug or a word of encouragement and needs to know there is more to life than feeling pain and discouragement because you came here to make a difference. You started out being loved and when that love turned into something you didn't recognize, you started to believe you weren't valuable. You started hurting yourself like others had hurt you and you thought that was how you were supposed to get through life. But I am here to tell you that the love you experienced a long time ago is still at the center of your being and just needs to be activated. There are people praying for you this very minute because you are worth caring about. So give yourself one more day, before you decide to leave, and see if the sun is shining or if it is just hiding behind a cloud before its glorious rays peek out and start to envelop the earth with its warmth and beauty. What good would it be if the sun decided that the clouds had just too much power and it just wasn't worth the effort to rise every morning, not knowing that so many people really do value the sun?

No one tells the sun how loved it is, but that doesn't mean it isn't thought of in a very special way. People can't give the sun value by telling it how wonderful it is.

It is wonderful anyway. And that is the truth about you. You might not hear it from others but it is true that you are valued for who you are. No one can come to this Earth without first being loved by God, which is an everlasting love that never dies. It just gets buried under emotional turmoil before it is ready to surface again. And the Universe is here to quietly support you by sending you exactly what you need...so open your heart and receive the energy that is directed at you in this moment because you matter!!!!.....

Is there someone else out there that feels ashamed because you participated in something you know was harmful to yourself and someone else because you didn't want to feel rejected? You went along with something that you know in your heart just wasn't right but you were afraid to speak up. The Universe wants you to know that you have not yet unleashed the power within you, but that day is here now for you to start saying "no" to the little things that trouble you before you can handle the big things. It is in saying "no" that will give you the freedom to unleash that power you already have but chose to bury it underneath fear, bondage, and dependency. When you go to the gym you start off slow to build your muscles before you can take on more. This is the same process for you.

Once your power is developed, you will never again return to the part of you that decided to be meek and afraid. God is waiting on you to use Him as your spiritual equipment. You will feel the love from Him after you say your first necessary "no" because you will be ready to let that love in that has been there for you right along. Don't be afraid to ask for what you need. You are truly loved for who you are not by your performance.

There is also someone out there who keeps themselves in "wanting" instead of "having." You are afraid of losing anything that you own, so consequently you either give it away, lose it, or get your needs met through everyone else. You have a habit of gambling because there's only a "chance" you could win, and then you will always have the opportunity to gamble your winnings away. And when you are not gambling, you are at the stores spending money. Yes, you have had quite a few losses in your life, but those losses were really opportunities to pull through as a victim or a victorious warrior. You chose to be a victim and the payoff was sympathy and pity, and others were willing to give you what you thought you needed through them, not anything that could last, because once again it wasn't yours. So you had to set up the next drama series so you could remind others you were still a victim. This existence is extremely sad and painful and the rewards are few. It's time to get in touch with the pain that you hold on to so that others feel sorry for you. The truth is you could have the steak you desire and not the crumbs that fall from other's plates. You could pull up a chair and sit at the same table as the ones you take from. You could get your own plate instead of waiting for someone else to finish theirs before you eat off their plate. You see, it's not that there is not a plate for you. For some reason you don't think you can make it on your own, and the Universe wants you to know, you are no different than the ones with the full bellies. It's time to claim your own and know that God is not out to get you. He has placed everything you need on this earth and you just have to be willing to receive it by letting go of the fear of losing or feeling rejected by others. The loss you hang on to is really the spring board to moving ahead. Everything in your life has happened for a reason and you can either use it for your benefit or use it to keep you down. If someone close to you died in your life…don't let it be for nothing. That death was also for your growth.

"Death" has the word "eat" in the center of it. Eat at the banquet table of life with your own plate filled!!!!

HAPPINESS

"Happiness happens when you happen to smile on happenings happening...."

Word Whisperer

In one of my meditations I asked the Universe to give me two questions that were meaningful and that most people would want to answer. What came to mind was the question "Are you Happy" and the next one was "What is happiness to you? I wanted to see how many people were really happy and if some of their explanations of happiness were the same as their experiences of happiness. I also wanted to see if the majority of answers were similar or were their several definitions of that one word. I did get permission to use their responses in this book. Here are some of the answers I received:

"Are you happy?" Stephanie said "I am."

"What does happiness mean to you?" Stephanie answered, "I haven't really thought about it. Living my life to the fullest...not sweating the small stuff. Pushing through....knowing I do the best I can for my son and I."

Same question about being happy and what happiness means to the following people:

Timmy G: "Sure"

"Happiness is getting along with people, enjoying life, doing what you want to do especially having a good time. No Stress...No strain. Letting life be.

Katie: "Yes."

"Peace of Mind."

Holley O.: "Yes." You can feel good in any situation. It's all perception and how you look at it."

Pat Y: "Did you have to ask me today? Not today. Happiness is fleeting."

"Happiness means when my family gets along and when I get along with my family. The sun shines and the birds sing and my kids and husband are happy."

Andy Y. "Sometimes I'm not and sometimes I am."

"To me, sustained happiness is not attainable because no matter what, you will have problems at times."

David M. "Yes."

"Happiness is a feeling I get when I am doing something I enjoy."

Jimmy D. "I guess....I don't know if anyone is. You have your moments."

"Happiness is being healthy, enjoying the little things...easier said than done."

Carol D. "I don't believe I am truly happy"

"Happiness is an inner thing...not outer. When you feel loved you have it all."

Theresa B. "Yes." Happiness is love, contentment, peace, and joy."

Michelle S. "Yes."

"Happiness is feeling content...not missing anything or wanting things to be different. Being satisfied with the way things are. No regrets."

Phil S. "Yes"

"Spending time with family and friends and being healthy."

MaryLou S. "Yes...very happy...."

"I think being surrounded by people you enjoy and who enjoy you and living in the Spirit of God to pass love around."

George S. "Yes..." I tell my wife, MaryLou, the best years of my life I spend with her."

"Happiness is when you find your destiny in life with the one you truly love. I thank God I found MaryLou. If heaven is like that it would be wonderful because I feel like I am in heaven now."

Dee O. "Yes"
"Happiness to me is a choice of how I want to look at things. I am only as happy as I choose to be."

Kevin O. "Yes" Living life in a positive way, enjoying life. Taking the best out of things. Making the best of everything.

Jamie S. M. "Very happy" "Loving the life you live."

Greg R. "Yes" Happiness means a lot of things to me. Being comfortable in life. Being with the person I love.

Bill R. "Yes" Happiness is a day of peace."

Bridget R. "Yes, I am happy."
"To be honest, happiness to me is loving who I am with."

Kaylei A. "Yes, very!
"Happiness means I am content with my life and the people in it. I surround myself with my family and boyfriend whom I adore."

Jordan A. "Yes. I am very happy and to me happiness is very extremely subjective. However, I believe it is the perfect balance of work and reward, and family and relaxation. With work comes stability and little financial worries, with family comes conformation, support, love, caring, and satisfaction that what you are doing in this life has purpose. Everyone wants to feel like they have a purpose in this world."

Brian G. "Oh yes!"
"Happiness, fulfillment, and contentment- when all these elements are in line with each other"....when everything is in order, my finances, food, health, connection to others and all living things. Contentment breeds happiness."

Alice H. "I am happy. There are times when your happiness can be affected by outside sources."
"Happiness is loving someone and knowing that person loves me."

Alexus O. "Right now? Yeah."
Happiness is like a beautiful landscape; like a fairy tale, magical, sparkly. Pink flowers, fluffy clouds like a cotton ball; Radiant.

Clinton B. "Yeah...Happiness means a nice bike ride on a sunny day, laying on the beach and no worries."

Ruth G. "Yes."
"Happiness is being content in situations I have in my life.
Accepting the things that come into my life without becoming bitter."

Bob G. "Sure, I'm happy.
"Happiness means that my family is cared for. That's it in a nutshell. I also have confidence when I die, I'm going to heaven."

Anthony "Yeah"
"Happiness is being with friends and loved ones and having fun."

Arianna G. "Yeah"
"Happiness is family, friends, and caring."

Jamie G: "Yes"
"Happiness means having a healthy, happy family ....that is what really matters to me in my life."

Evan R. "Yes."
"I would say happiness means freedom from worries. A light mind...no heavy thoughts and no stress........a stress free environment."

Phil S. "Yes."
"Happiness means being healthy and happy. I have a good family."

Matthew G. "Yes."
"I would say happiness is knowing I have a relationship with Jesus and when I die, my eternity is secure. My family being healthy is happiness too."

Kathy W. "I am happy. Happiness is being around good friends and being peaceful."

Kathy C. "I am happy sometimes. Happiness would be to be alone and healthy."

Lyman M. "I am happy. Life is happiness."

Steven G. "Yes".....Happiness is being healthy, having friends and family and earning my keep. Also respect from family and friends and love from them and being married to Sue who takes care of my family in ways I might not think of."

Sue G. "Yes"... Inner peace, family and friends and trying to make the world better by being a good friend and taking care of the Earth...and of course Steve, my daughter and all of the family."

Ralph B. "Yes".....Happiness is my toys, traveling and being with Ardith"
It is fascinating how everyone has a different definition of the same word. One word....different perceptions. Isn't that just like life?

I SEE WITH THE EYES OF GOD

"We have two eyes so we can see more and only one mouth so we can say less."

Word Whisperer

Eve was sitting in a corner in the garden.
"Lord, I have a problem."
"What's the problem, Eve?"
"I know that you created me and provided this beautiful garden and all of these wonderful animals, as well as that hilarious comedic snake, but I'm just not happy.
"And why is that Eve?"
"Lord, I am lonely, and I'm sick to death of apples."
Well, Eve, in that case, I have a solution; I shall create a man for you."
"Man?" "What is that Lord?"
He's a flawed creature, with many bad traits. He'll lie, cheat, and be vain; all in all, he'll give you a hard time. But he'll be bigger, faster, and will like to hunt and kill things. I'll create him in such a way that he will satisfy your physical needs. He will be witless, and will revel in childish things like fighting and kicking a ball about. He won't be as smart as you, so he will also need your advice to think properly."
Sounds great," says Eve, with raised eyebrows, "but what's the catch Lord?"
"Well, you can have him on one condition."
"And what's that Lord?"
"As I said, he'll be proud, arrogant, and self-admiring, so you'll have to let him believe that I made him first. And it will have to be our little secret...you know....woman to woman."
Ok...I had to share this joke just for laughs and to show you how perception can certainly be used in different ways. You have to admit, the punch line will get you every time... It's like the elections coming up this year and I see so many people divided on their choice of candidates. I always wonder how so many people

can see so differently. If one person is supposed to be so wonderful, then why can't everyone agree on the same candidate? Why can't other people see what you see? Then it dawned on me that we all see what we want to see in any given case. I mean, if good can be assigned to both parties, and it always is, then that might be seeing with the eyes of God. I know it's hard to like them both when you are supposed to pick one over the other, but what fascinates me is how the world perceives two different people in so many different ways. Some love one and some love the other.

Does that mean they are both lovable even if I can't see that correlation in my world? How is it that one can see so clearly as to why they like the one they choose, but it is not clear to another when they have the same facts in front of them? How is it someone else can see what you can't see even when they state their opinions on their own facts? Now, in order to understand perspective, I would have to remove myself from the whole situation and look at it from afar. Is that how God would operate? Take off the judgments and just see two people in a loving light? Do you really have to have opposition in order to really like something? I see it in the sports arena all the time. You choose one opponent over the other, but once again someone else is for the opposing team. Then there is that particular person you don't care for but other people like him or her. It can be the same person, same facts, but different opinions. How complex is the mind? Is that how we create our realities, not necessarily on what is, but more on opinions and judgments? Obviously. You have to have a judgment to have an opposing view. What would happen if you took the judgment out of the mix? Would you then be able to like both parties? Is that even a possibility?

Is that why God is supposed to be capable of "unconditional love" and we as humans might not be capable of such a thing?

I remember hearing a statement one time that could take the sting out of any situation. It was "If it won't matter in a hundred years, it shouldn't matter now." In other words the things you think are so important right now, won't even exist someday. The A's or F's on your report card will be long gone and you will have to find your way according to your own needs not your performances. When I graduated from high school and went back several years later to view the building, it amazed me how meaningless it was after it had so much meaning at one time in my life. The studying, the tests, the teachers, the friendships and romances, and now, I stood looking at a building that had no meaning, just past memories that didn't satisfy my hunger in the present. A kind of sadness took place, knowing that I couldn't get back my past. I might recreate similarities but never the same exact duplicate. That's why some judgments keep you from experiencing the full meaning of life. You might put too much emphasis on an outside condition or you might put love on hold and use anger instead, blocking any good thing that might come your way.

When you go to sleep at night you are in a relaxed state of mind and this is because you are in a state of suspended judgment. This is where you get your peace and can rest your mind and body. And let's talk about black and white issues. I don't know about you, but when I look at the color white in terms of crayons, or a white piece of paper and then I look at the color of my skin, I can honestly say my skin does not look white. White to me is chalk white and I have never seen anyone walking around with chalk white skin unless they were ill. But our minds are conditioned to a certain judgment of "white" so we accept that we are white. The mind is fascinating at best. I do understand where some judgment is necessary but I think the key is not to put such emphasis on the judgment to make room for more love in your life. I know for me, I continually take off my earth glasses and try to see with the eyes of God as much as I possibly can.

Nadia Ohar

IS IT REALLY ABOUT THE MONEY

"Financial affairs are the doors to success;
Money won't stay if your life is a mess;
Clean up your act if you want to have more;
There's never a good reason for you to stay poor..."

Word Whisperer

After having done the survey on "happiness," I am happy to say that it doesn't sound like it is about the money. Most people want to be healthy and some people say they don't think you can stay happy, but no one really said I would be happy if I had money. So what that tells me is people don't really believe that money is the main reason for happiness even though you might hear it said "if only I had money, I would be all set." Our spirit knows that it isn't the money that makes us happy, because when everyone answered the "happiness" question money wasn't even mentioned. The evidence is astonishing when you think that at least one person would have said "money."

When you look at what money can buy, it seems like that would be all you would need to be happy. You pay your bills, you buy extra toys for yourself, you could travel the world, and you could probably even buy an illusion of love. But what I have learned is, you have to be happy first before you have the money. If you are not happy, then nothing you buy can sustain happiness. First off, after you leave the store, your item starts becoming old and after it is used it doesn't have the same affect that it had the first time because the "newness" wears off. It is like that with new cars, new relationships, new shoes, etc. "New" seems to last for a very short time.

When talking with one of my daughters, she made a good point. She said other than food and shelter, we really don't have a need for anything else. Most everything else is just a "want." And lf the truth be told, if "God supplies all our needs" then we have to understand that some of the important things are free. If we love one another, then we are in a give and take relationship that automatically flows with some of our needs. There is too much emphasis on working too many hours just to "get by." Unavailability creeps in and all the money in the world won't make up for your missing body. You need to be present in the relationship and money is no substitute for human contact.

I always feel good when a client comes in and "walks their path" and finds satisfaction in hearing what will uplift and help them in their life. Money is nice but it can't buy the feeling that comes with seeing someone feel good about themselves. There is nothing wrong with charging someone for a service you give them, as long as your intent isn't set on just making money. It's been said to do what you love and the money will follow. Most people aren't able to get in touch with their gifts and talents because they are so busy working for someone else, that they just don't have the time or energy to find their own gifts. And even if you recognize what your gifts are, you may find a reason why you can't afford to use them to the fullest.

I know for me, I tried working for others and I always came to the same place. There was always a time for me to leave and it was in the "in between" time that I was able to find my gifts and make money doing them. Had I continued to work on the outside, I would never have discovered some of the creative works that flowed through me. I was making "preventive flu packets," "plaques with meaning", "tributes," bracelets, etc. all using my writing and computer skills. So anytime you leave your job, whether it be your decision, or maybe you are fired or laid off, see the gift in having time to discover more about yourself. Before I understood that the Universe was for me and that everything that happens in my life was for a good reason, I would get angry and bring myself to tears when something didn't go the way I thought it should. I felt I always had a struggle with money issues and never having enough, before I understood that all my needs were met. I didn't really need all the things I thought I needed. I wasn't going to die without dessert with my meal, or if "Show Time" had to be left off the cable list. I found I enjoyed listening to music much more than watching TV anyway. Just another discovery about who I really was. And I didn't care what type of car I drove, as long as it had heat in the winter and air conditioning in the summer.

If you take a look at your basic needs, you might find you are probably well off. If you remove all the political and religious movements out of your life, and decide to think for yourself what kind of life you want to build, you would have more of a chance doing it yourself than having to rely on some stranger on the outside. Promises are just like sand castles in the air with no foundation to support or uphold any of the well-spoken words that can go by the way side. Why not feel good about your life without looking for someone else to make it better. You will probably never have the opportunity to talk face-to-face with a politician and state your personal needs anyway. Bring it to God where there is a chance that He is listening. After all, if you believe, you don't have to run out of your house to find Him…He will find you.

I also want to touch on the idea that money, while it just looks like it's a separate entity in your life, it is really a symbol of how you treat your relationships. In other words, if money was a person, you would have the same relationship with this money, as you do with the relationships in your life. If you are afraid to be close in a relationship, you might have a lot of money before scarcity sets in. Money is a relationship and if you want more of it, you have to change the relationship you have with it right now. I would suggest you do this exercise. Pull up an empty chair in front of you and place money in the form of a bill on that chair. Prop it up on a pillow so you can be at eye level. It doesn't matter whether it is a one dollar bill or a fifty dollar bill; just that it is sitting there in front of you. I want you to take a deep breath and let it out. Do that two more times before you start this exercise. Now I want you to get real and talk to your money as if you were talking to a friend in front of you. Tell your money all the reasons you have not been a good friend and how sorry you are that you treated your money like it wasn't important and share your fears with this money about how you were afraid to let it in because you didn't want to be hurt if you weren't in total control of how and when your money came and went. Tell your money that you are angry because you feel it let you down at the times when you needed it the most and you closed your heart to being hurt again. At this time ask the money for your forgiveness for the way you shut it out of your life, and how you blamed the money instead of taking responsibility for your part in the relationship. Let whatever feelings you have come up and let them go. You are making peace in this relationship and you are no longer going to block the flow of money into your life. Now, physically, pick up your money and place it on your heart and let it know how much you love and appreciate having it in your life. Be thankful for the new relationship that is now in place that will benefit you both. Your money will not only bless you but will be used as a blessing to others. Not only will money help you with your purpose in life, but you have helped money find its purpose in the world.

While we are on the topic of money, I remember writing a few chapters on the most expensive holiday of the year. The day when you lie to your children about a stranger coming into your house with all kinds of gifts that you worked hard to buy. You actually teach your children there are flying reindeer and there is a man who is going to get into their home and come down the chimney. Now, I am not pointing fingers at anyone, because I have to be honest. I did the same thing as everyone else. I wanted to get my children everything they wanted on that day and didn't mind going into debt to do it. So for one day of a holiday that was filled with instant gratification, I struggled financially for the rest of the year until the season was upon me once again. Through my writing about Christmas, I was finally able to see the light in a humorous manner. I want to share a few chapters from that book with you now starting with the disappearing Christmas tree. Now you see it....now you don't......get ready for truth with a tinge of entertainment before the holidays begin.

OH CHRISTMAS TREE

I am a strong and sturdy evergreen;
Big strong limbs that you've ever seen;
I sway to and fro to the beat of the breeze;
Snow on my limbs, you'd think I'd freeze;

But it's not like that in the woods for me;
The weather's my friend, not my enemy;
I have bonded with storms as they come;
It's the person who comes for my trunk, I shun;

I know it's Christmas and nowhere to run;
The human wants me for his daughter or son;
The water that falls is really not from the dew;
They are just the tears that are caused by you;

Each time you slice me with your ax;
You kill a life and that's the facts;
I don't mean to ruin your holiday;
It's just that trees should have a say......

Word Whisperer

When I think of all the activity that takes place in picking out
the "perfect" tree, not to mention the expense, I can understand why
you breathe a sigh of relief when it is over. The decorations, the tree
lights, tree stand, ornaments, tree top, etc. can be very costly and
expensive this time of year. By the time you are done buying gifts,
you don't have enough money to buy the sale items after the
holidays where it is an illusion you can save money.

Now this tree can drink quite a bit of water if your tree is real
but thank God water is free. I do not understand why trees don't
come with adoption papers considering the way they are fussed over
and taken into the family like another child.

I mean…think about it…. Let's look at this tree ordeal through the eyes of an innocent child. Everything in the world has a place. INSIDE the house you have your couch, TV, kitchen table, potty chair, beds, etc. OUTSIDE you have your sidewalks, cars, streetlights and TREES. Then for some unknown reason, a grown adult, whom you believe to be a lot smarter than any kid, comes strolling into the house huffing and puffing and dragging almost forcibly, a tree over their shoulder. Confusion sets in, but the child gives the adult the benefit of the doubt. But it doesn't end here. This bare tree is brought into this child's home like a newborn out of the womb. The family gives it a place of its own and then starts to nurture it. Everyone gathers around and starts dressing this tree with ornaments, lights, and admiration. It is fed water and becomes a central part of the family. Every morning, the child runs to this beautiful creation and even shrugs off the idea that trees belong outdoors. The child's heart wells up with love and makes room in his life for this new addition. The child may not have been able to talk his parents into having a pet, but now he has the next best thing. He has formed an attachment to this tree. Not only does this tree add a glorious touch to the room, but here is where all the presents are to be placed. A symbol of pure happiness! Life is good…tree lights at night…some blinking, some just sparkling like diamonds in the wind. Anticipation sets in as the night get closer to the big happening! This tree is just so special! The small o-o-h's and a-a-h-h's are just a confirmation of how this young child feels about the new addition to the family. Then it happens…Christmas is over and Daddy and Mommy decide the tree is no longer useful, and if you can believe this one…they throw it out! Cast aside like it never existed in the first place! Anxiety sets in…if they can throw away something they grew to love and admire, what happens to me? What if they get tired of me? These are just some of the thoughts this young child has to deal with. Here we have a situation where the child is now afraid based on the senseless actions of his parents whom he is supposed to trust and find guidance. The child has fears of not being able to meet his parent's expectations and could grow up with a pattern of not trying to succeed at anything because if this tree couldn't make it with all its glory, then what would be the use of trying? Failure sets in and a defeated pattern is formed.

Okay, maybe I do get carried away with this Christmas thing but one more thing before I move on. Trees belong outside in their own surroundings. They like the outdoors. How would you like to be snatched out of your own home and put outdoors just because a tree wanted you for their selfish needs? Hey what comes around goes around...be careful! I'm only trying to help. There's more. "You better watch out...You better not pout...Santa's coming to town! HE SEES YOU WHEN YOU'RE SLEEPING HE KNOWS WHEN YOU'RE AWAKE....HE KNOWS IF YOU'VE BEEN GOOD OR BAD." I mean is there no privacy!?!? These poor children walking around turning into little neurotics analyzing everything they do at such a young age. And these grown adults who take advantage of such a delicate situation. "That's it...Santa's not coming....you really screwed up this time!" Then five minutes later..."That's it...Santa's not bringing you any toys." I wonder how many times Santa is not coming. Talk about a power play. Make your kid behave by using Santa as a weapon, doing more harm than good.

Oh sure, parents have a moment of instant gratification when the child obeys because he wants toys from Santa. But what happens when the holidays are over and the parents are on their own? Good luck with that. What threat can top Santa? The Easter Bunny is no big deal. Candy is an everyday thing in a kid's life. The tooth fairy is no threat. And what about the other fears that pop up this time of year? The young children who are afraid of Santa and are told that even locked doors won't stop him because he comes down the chimney. He is getting in come hell or high water!!! And to add insult to injury, parents want you to leave Santa some cookies. That's right...reward him for breaking and entering. Talk about feeling unprotected.

And what about the disappointments you have to contend with on such a glorious day? You tell your children that Santa is bringing the gifts so kids think they can order anything they want because after all, money is no object. You just have to be good to get what you want. Then it happens. Little Johnny doesn't get the big drums he asked for, or Susie doesn't get the giant Barbie House she wrote on her list. Confusion sets in. These children start feeling like they did something wrong or they are not good enough. They have "stuffed" their true feelings all season long and now they don't get rewarded. Anger mounts and they are not grateful for what they did get. Of course the parents can't understand why their children are never happy. And the beat goes on even without the drums. Okay…I am just trying to help you save money. How am I doing? There's more!

What about the families that have the brothers and sisters involved. They always compare how many presents they each received. Never mind Johnny's presents cost more, so he got less. Children have no idea about expense and besides there is no expense when we are talking about Satan…umm I mean Santa. Okay one more story.

My story regarding the Christmas holidays would not be complete if I didn't talk about December birthdays. Instead of buying a birthday card for the recipient, I now buy a sympathy card and it is never questioned. I mean, let's face it. When your parents buy you a birthday gift in December, how do you know you're not really getting one of your Christmas gifts? Talk about getting cheated out of a holiday. Try and throw a birthday party in December and see how many people don't show. But the good news in all of this is, for the first five years of your child's life, you can actually skip their birthday and just have Christmas. They are not going to know it's their birthday as long as you don't tell them. It is harder to skip Christmas because everyone celebrates that holiday. But a birthday is a little less conspicuous. Think of all the money you can save for the first five years of their life with no birthday presents, no expensive parties. Whatever you saved, you can use after they turn five. Remember, they can't miss what they haven't had, but once you start, there is no turning back!

Another important tip to remember for December birthdays is to make sure you don't use Christmas wrapping paper for a birthday party just because it is in the house and convenient to use at the time. I made the mistake of sending my son to a birthday party with Christmas wrap and the kid he gave the present to put it under the tree and then demanded a birthday present. My son would not leave me alone until I took him to the store to pick out a birthday present for his buddy. Live and learn!

There is a perfect solution to all this madness. Everyone who is born in December, move his or her birthday up a month or move it back to

November. Last names beginning with the letters "A through N" will have their birthday in November and "M through Z" will have to take January. There are rules to everything in life. HAPPY CHRISTMAS AND MERRY BIRTHDAY TO ALL!!!

I showed you the humorous side of Christmas but now I want to share the more serious side. Why do we all 'pretend" it's everybody's birthday on Christmas? Do we do it because everyone else does it? What would happen if we all took a stand and decided that Christmas had been blown way out of proportion and now it is time to run Santa out of town? We are grown people telling lies to our kids by telling them something is real when it isn't. We go out of our way to prove this lie by bringing our kids to see Santa Claus. There is physical evidence supplied. How confusing it must be when we say there is no Santa when they've seen him with their own eyes. And if they have ever sat on his lap and gave him their list of toys, they have established a relationship with him. If you can't trust your parents then who can you trust. Let's face it...we "do" Christmas to make our kids and everyone else happy but we pay a price. Think about it. Candy and cookies make them happy too, but it also can make them fat, ruin their teeth, and make them hyper, etc. It's understandable why we ignore the negative results because it takes time to get fat or grow a cavity, the same way it takes time for anger and trust issues to build into patterns. Did you ever stop and wonder why there are so many suicides and people with depression right after the holiday? Ironically, Christmas with all the expense, is held at the coldest time of the year when the heating and oil bills are due. Don't you think it would be a great idea to add the figures of what you spend on needless presents and figure out what bills you could pay instead. Gee, wouldn't that be a nice start to a new year. One other thing before I get off the subject of

Christmas. My heart goes out to the families with more than one child. The pressure of trying to buy for one is bad enough. Multiply that pressure by two or more and it can be very depressing. Kids have friends and friends compare and parents pay the price. No one wants to come up short on this deal. Taking on Christmas is like taking on a Giant, without the slingshot, or a storm without shelter. On some level I think this all needed to be said and if it helps even one person to do it a little different this year, than someone will be enjoying the holidays a whole lot more. If the season is more about "giving," then how about giving more of your time to someone or giving more love than you normally do, or giving away items you don't use anymore. These are free and meaningful experiences, but not an expense. And by staying out of the malls, you will find time to make use of your gifts and talents and get creative in whatever you choose to give.

TAKE AUTHORITY OVER YOUR LIFE

Sometimes you need to be your own best friend;
Especially when your heart is on the mend;
Who else would know you better than you?
You are strong enough to make it through......

Word Whisperer

Today I woke up with something interesting on my mind. It's not that I had a strange dream or anything but it was a sense of being able to take control of my life. Not just taking the back seat and going along for the ride, which by the way was something I was used to doing. When you are a passenger and not the driver, you basically are navigating on someone else's compass. You get to your destination on their time schedule and you don't necessarily have a say in how the trip unfolds. Now if that's you, it's not too late to move into the driver's seat. There are rewards for taking control of your life. You actually have a say and you even feel good about your destination because it's something you planned. You get to experience what it's like to matter!!! You get to exercise that part of the brain that has to make decisions and it's not so scary once you realize there are no wrong choices, but just opportunities to experience. I know in the past, I surrounded myself with very powerful people and I allowed their power to intimidate me so I would not stand up for myself when opinions were stated as facts. Come on, you know some of the people in your life that state their opinions as facts and you don't dare state yours unless you agree with their opinions. Well I am here to support and encourage you to a way out without having to get rid of everyone in your life. First of all, I believe we all agree to play roles in our lives and if you are intimidated by anyone at all, you chose to play the timid role because you were rewarded in some way by the other person. Either you were approved of because you didn't speak up or you got a chance to think badly of yourself because you acted like a mouse instead of a lion. Either way, roles can change when you decide. It's like playing a part in a movie as a certain character, and you become known as that type of character. It is hard to switch roles, but you just need to take on another script and practice that one until you decide if that works for you. None of us were born leaders or followers. We were just born. Then, somewhere along the way, you decided what role worked for you. I can honestly say I feel like a leader, but I took on the role as a follower. For me, it just seemed easier and more convenient to let someone else do the work and I would accept whatever came my way. I practiced not taking charge of my life, and took the easy way out. When I look at the long term effects of doing that, I see the damage that has been done. Most of the leaders in my life have marriage partners, houses, and have no problem setting goals. I, on the other hand, have an apartment building where "they" take care of everything if you have a problem. The only thing about living in an apartment is there is very little privacy and you don't get to enjoy the outdoors like you would in your own private yard. Someone else has the final say even though you pay good money to live there. But the good news is that it is never too late to change something that is not working. I highly recommend starting with a goal and then taking small steps to achieve it. This book is a good example. I have a deadline to meet, and my goal is to write something every day. I do not worry about how much I get done because once my thoughts are in order the words just flow. Once I achieve my goal, I will find another goal to finish even if it's something small. Goals don't have to be long term or even monstrous in size. Getting up in the morning and meditating might be a goal. Or you can even go for a walk a few times a week. Whatever you decide, just make sure you follow through. I believe the "follow through" is just as important as the goal is to accomplish. Without the "follow through" you mine as well forget about the goal. At one time in my life I was so used to everyone completing what I needed done, that when I was left on my own, I could only get half the work done and never realized why I couldn't complete anything. This is why it is so harmful to step in and do everything for someone else because you pretend they are not capable so you can fill your own needs to feel needed by someone else. The people in your life that are being taken care of might like that role for a while but they will have the same "follow through" issues waiting for someone else to finish what they once started. I live by myself, make my own decisions and I seem self-sufficient but the truth is by carrying the pattern of having others do the things for me that I should have been doing for myself, I still leave dishes in the sink. I might do some of the dishes but decide to soak the others. For some reason, I do not want to complete anything, even if it was just the dishes. Maybe it's because it gave me the illusion that I still had a purpose. But the good news is I am still in the process of changing my role, and I can't wait to see all the chores I do get done, eventually.

Then there is the authority you take over pain or sickness in your life. If you go by the bible, you can plead the blood of Jesus over your situation. If you are not familiar with doing that, you might understand that you are a Divine Being and you affirm your good health and your right to be healthy by affirming "There is no sickness in the Divine plan for my life. Therefore, I have faith in the goodness of life and remove all fear-based thoughts that block the goodness that is mine to claim. I receive the healing energy of love and thank God for my abundant life. And so it is!" I suggest you write these affirmations down and keep them in sight so you can renew your mind. It is also important to remember that most of the problems in our life are just illusions because the only way you can experience anything other than goodness is when you step out of the "truth." Truth will correct all errors in the mind. Truth has the perfect gift of love which does not falter in the face of pain. This is the gift of healing, for the truth needs no defense and therefore attack cannot take place. Use the same truths to take authority over your finances and start by being grateful for what you have and the act of being thankful will always bring you more of what you want. I don't suggest focusing all your attention on "getting" money because there are a whole lot of areas in your life that cover the "abundance" need and that includes money but doesn't make money the exclusive objective. In fact money is not the issue. It's just an exchange of paper. When you make it the issue you are actually hiding the real cause of lack which could be "undeserving," "unworthy" or "unlovable" thoughts about yourself. Make sure you use the words "worthy," "deserving" and "lovable" in your daily affirmation. This affirmation may help in the area of finances. "I align myself with truth and integrity and allow myself to receive the blessings I so deserve. There is a continuous movement of supply, money and all that I need to express life fully and I am open to receiving my good. I am perfect, whole and complete and I deserve all the goodness life has to offer." Forgiveness is also necessary to make room for your "highest good." There is no justification that can cover the damage that un-forgiveness brings into your life. You are not hurting the other person by holding on to anger and resentment. You are hurting yourself. I am sure you have heard it said that when you hold on to resentment and bitterness it's like drinking poison and hoping the other person will die from it. It just can't happen. So now that you know it doesn't serve you, are you ready to take on an affirmation that might help? "I know in order to truly love myself, I need to forgive myself and others for any and all imperfections that created pain in my life. I allow myself to "let go" of expectations and accept myself at all levels, knowing, that every experience is always for my highest good. I accept "what is" and allow the healing to take place. I am loved!" Remember to copy these affirmations and say them daily. Congratulations for taking your life back and living it to the fullest! You deserve the best!

THE PROBLEM WITH YOUR LIFE IS.......

THERE IS NO PROBLEM

"There is an ounce of prevention against hate and dissension, if you set your intention to focus attention on love...not to mention it relieves all tension"

Word Whisperer

Did you know that problems are just made up stories that our brain conceives of something as being wrong. I cannot tell you how many times I have run "worry" thoughts over and over in my mind until I would experience the actual feelings that went along with that "worry." Even if the outcome was not as I perceived it, I still had the results of a bad outcome from being afraid. It wasn't until I really understood the power of the mind that I actually decided to take those "worry" thoughts and change it into a "like" something about the situation. How many of you know you cannot hold two thoughts at the same time in your mind? When I would start to worry about not having a car, I changed my thoughts to how nice a new car would feel once it became a reality. I didn't bring in the low energy thoughts about how could I afford a new car or how long was it going to take to manifest? No...No...No... I stayed with uplifting thoughts that served me and made me feel good. If I started worrying about any of my children, I would focus on all the reasons they had to be happy. And the truth is, you can always find one thing you can like about any situation. Even if you are married and you have a disagreement, you can turn your thoughts to something you like about your husband or wife. Even pain or sickness has a good side to it. It might cause you to take better care of yourself or to slow down and smell the coffee. If your furnace breaks down and the cold sets in, you might want to bring warm thoughts to your mind, and get excited about the fact there is no such thing as being cold forever. "This too shall pass" is a tool for getting through anything that feels uncomfortable. Just keep pouring good thoughts into your mind. Even when you lose a loved one and are experiencing the loss, you can always remind yourself that they are in a better place and they are not in pain anymore. One day you will reconnect with them in the Spirit world where you once were before you manifested into this world. I am not suggesting you bury your feelings because the truth is, your feelings have a mind of their own and do not leave until you let them go. I will tell you this, you are in charge of how long you want to feel bad. If you find you can't sleep at night, I would recommend some soft music so at least you are relaxing. Or you can write in your journal if that is appealing to you. The key is to find some type of enjoyment while you are awake. It doesn't serve you to run all kinds of thoughts in your mind about the things you did not get done, or all the chores that are waiting to be done the next day. There really is nothing wrong with NOT worrying. It doesn't mean you don't care. It just means you care more about being happy than you do about being miserable. Try it. Think of something that makes you happy. It might take some of you a few minutes but that's okay. Once that happy thought arises, hold it in place until your body feels the benefit of that pleasant thought. Be aware of how your body seems to relax and feel lighter when you think good thoughts. Practice that happiness thought throughout your day, and I promise you, your day will be filled with even more happiness. Remember, you are like a magnet and you will draw in wherever your thoughts take you. You will see the manifestation of either pleasure or pain. If you are thinking of a nice vacation spot where you know you would love to go, your feelings might even match actually being there right now. When I think of my new car I want to manifest, I can feel the same excitement as if it were already sitting in my parking space. But believe me, that takes practice so don't get discouraged if your feelings don't automatically match your good thoughts. You don't walk into a gym for the first time and come out of the place like you've been there for a year. Like anything new, it takes getting used to. Especially all you professional "worriers", and you know who you are. If you are a parent it will really be an adjustment on your part. I remember when when my kids were out driving at night and my whole body would remain tense until they arrived home safely. I would picture all the things that could happen, especially if it was snowing or the roads were icy. I would run around letting my kids know just how awful it was out there so I could scare them into being careful. My favorite saying was always "Be careful!" I didn't know that kind of talk could hold them back in their lives when they got older. I was teaching them there was something to be afraid of even if they couldn't see what it was. Now, I let them know "You are fine!" I didn't know at that time to send thoughts of love their way and affirm their safety and protection through prayer and positive thinking. I now understand how the Universe gets the imprint of your thoughts and delivers back to you, your own requests. I was afraid so I would get the manifestation of something to be afraid of. It just reinforced my need to be right and keep my beliefs in place. If you worry, the Universe will honor your requests. The Universe doesn't try and figure it out any more than a garden stresses out about the seeds you plant. The garden doesn't say you should have more of this or less of that, but just gives you the results of your seeds planted. And that is how the Universe works. It gives you back the results of your thoughts you planted so get ready for your harvest. How empowering is it for you to know you can change your life by planting your thoughts in ways that will benefit you. And the good news is thoughts are free and available at all times to all people on this planet. That's how good God is. You came equipped to live a good life without having to do anything more than use your words wisely. Your thoughts will remain with you until the day you die. Why not embrace them and make peace with them so you both can work together as partners and not strangers. It is interesting how we think we are dealing with people on this earth but the truth is we are actually dealing with thoughts. Our relationships are built on other people's thoughts and conversation is always made up of thoughts first and then words spoken. So ironically we are just vehicles for the thoughts to have a life of their own. Why not be the Limo or the Rolls Royce rather than the broken down vehicle for your thoughts to travel in? You like to travel in style and so do your thoughts. Next time you have an issue against someone in your life, just realize it's not the person. It's the thoughts that are traveling with that person. You wouldn't get mad at your vehicle you are driving or stop and tell it off because you did not like something and when you are mature enough you will be able to view people the same way. After all, it's the thought that counts!!!!

ENERGY POWERED WORDS

Loving you is not always easy to do;
It's a gift I've chosen to give to you;
There's no conditions, no being right;
It's the God in me that holds you tight...

Word Whisperer

Words carry vibrations according to the meanings assigned to each word. Even certain foods contain lower and higher vibrations. Sweets, sugar, alcohol, and other low energy foods carry a low vibration and when you put that into your body, your body maintains that frequency as long as that food remains in your body. I did a chapter on different colors of food and each color carries a certain vibration that you will put into your body and match the frequency of that food. Higher frequency foods give your body a higher vibration level and the opportunity to draw in that same vibration level which includes money, people, and other items. This is why it is so important to recognize the vibrations in your environment. If you smoke, or drink, be prepared to draw in low vibration situations or items that come into your life. People with losing patterns will also show up at your doorstep. You might exercise, eat right, and live a disciplined and stable life, and your outer world should be reflecting good things with a healthy pattern. Words you use have meaning according to a 'collective consciousness," which means that the meaning behind the words you speak carry a vibration of millions of other people's thoughts. It's like turning up the voltage when you speak them. Energy is used in everything we say, do and have. Like food, there are certain words that vibrate at higher frequencies. The word "Jesus" resonates at a high frequency and is often used in healings and spreading love to others. Anytime you bring "love" into a situation, a certain type of healing always takes place. High frequency words such as "Divine," "Spirit," "God," are always useful in improving your life or "lifting" yourself to another level. Prayer is most effective when you are in a state of thankfulness before you get what you are asking for. It is important that you do not beg for things to happen. That implies you are doubtful and uncertain. It is better if you use "affirmative prayer" in any situation as you state your wishes as if you already have the end result. You do not need to see the evidence first. You bring the invisible into the visible. You don't look at the problem. You look at the solution. Some people get stuck in the problem and don't realize they can turn up the "voltage" by using the right words to ensure the proper results. Oh yes…we create the problems by first using low frequency thoughts and words. Electricity can't work unless you plug into something. Picture yourself with a plug attached to your body. What do you want to plug into? If it's God or a Higher Power, take your plug and visualize plugging into the main socket and connecting to all the power there is. Plug into the people around you that encourage, support and bring you the "good news" about life. Know when to "unplug" at any given moment. Remember, your participation is part of an end result. It doesn't pay to get over heated in any discussion because you could blow a fuse and when I say blow a fuse, I mean you could electrocute a part of your body that needs to continue functioning in order for you to live a full life here on Earth. How does it feel to be born a certified electrician? The umbilical cord was merely a plug into a source that kept you alive but when that cord was cut, it gave you the opportunity to have your own invisible plug. When I feel pain in my body, I know I am getting too much voltage from the thoughts I am carrying around with me. It's a warning sign just like smoke is before a fire. Oh yes, we always get warning signs first, and if we fail to acknowledge them and continue on in the same manner, then the signs just keep getting bigger and bigger before we have to listen. Do you realize that everything carries energy, from the clothes on your back to the car that you drive? The clothes you choose to wear each day can either uplift you, or bring you down. It's very important to pay attention to the colors you wear because each individual color carries a vibration of their own. Red carries the lowest rate of vibration. It is an expression of vitality and is also a very passionate color. If you choose orange, it is an expression of success. When you wear this color it helps expand your interest and activities. Yellow is a creative color and motivates you to action.

Blue represents maturity, calmness and dependability. Green is a vibrant color of life and growth. So you see, once again, everything has meaning. From the words you speak, to the thoughts you think, to the foods you eat and the colors you dress yourself with. A lot of your choices are made without a lot of thought behind them. I know when I picked out clothes to wear, I didn't give anything a second thought unless I chose something to keep me warm. That was the extent of my knowledge about the meaning associated with color. Then I started getting interested in meanings behind the scenes. In other words I had to know why things happen the way they do and what makes them happen this way and what does it all mean? I always loved bright colors and I can honestly say, I still do to this day. I use them in my work with clients when they walk their path. I have different color therapy glasses that they can choose from before they start their path adventure. I make colored bracelets with meaning behind each one. I have always been led to use my creative talents in such a way that each person would leave the session feeling good about their life with tools to keep growing daily. God is truly a God of color!!!

Nadia Ohar

LETTING GO

In order to begin you might have to end;
It could be an old pattern or maybe a friend;
Sometimes it's hard when you try and let go;
The old is familiar, the new you don't know...

Word Whisperer

I never understood the importance of "letting go" as much as I do now. To me "letting go" was vague and unimportant. I mean, if you didn't map out what I needed to let go of, then it could mean anything. Was it a person, place or thing? Was it taking the garbage out at night? Or was it something you had to use your mind first and then the letting go would follow. What I am realizing now, is that we all have a past we need to let go of sometime along the way. Our present is filled with everything we bring from the past. Faces change, places change, but the past remains the same. If your parents drank or were on drugs, chances are you drink or do drugs. If you don't, then someone you are involved with probably does. One way or another, you will have it in your life. If there was abuse in your past, guess what your future will contain? Poverty might be a past issue brought into the present. However your past was, rest assured you get to live it over again unless you decide you want it to be different. Then you "let go!" That means you stand up to the pain or whatever else comes up for you when you allow yourself to confront the issues you are facing today. Get rid of the blame, stop the anger, and feel the pain so you can move on. Forgiveness is key because when you get to that point, you are not holding on to resentment and bitterness that will harm you more than that person did from your past. There is no going around or climbing over what you have been avoiding. I know for me, I thought I could rise above everything and nothing would affect me. But then I would have big things happen such as the loss of my job, or not enough money to pay the rent when I had small children, or my marriage would fall apart. Everything was always BIG in my life because I would not deal with the small things first. I couldn't run away from my feelings because they would always catch up with me. Listen, I understand why people don't want to deal. I wouldn't raise my hand if someone said "who wants to feel pain so you can feel better later?" But the truth is, there is no other way because that pain is with you every day. You are actually harboring it inside of you and have a relationship with it daily. The pain helps you stay insecure and doesn't allow for you to be vulnerable because that would be a release and pain has made a home in you. Listen, if you carried a big stone with you every day, believe me, you would miss it if you left it home accidentally. It's because you are familiar with the past and you are familiar with your actions that lead you into the same results you experienced one time or another in your past. In other words, what you are familiar with, you might keep, just because it's something you know. Most of the time, "letting go" brings you to that spot where you are not familiar with what is next. You don't know what is going to happen next because you've never been down that road. You have to be willing to venture where no man as gone before. Even if someone did take that path before you, you still would have different results because no two people are the same. I was watching my grandson Carter learning how to walk, and I saw his resistance to "letting go" of the chair he was holding on to so he could take a step forward. I coaxed him to do it and after a few minutes of holding out my hands to him, he finally let go and took a step. What a proud moment!!!! I would like to think there is always a cheering squad for each and every one of us, even if we can't see into the invisible, because our spirit knows we can do what it takes for us to move forward and our spirit has a connection to the Divine. We have to stop thinking we are alone and that the world is a scary place to live. You feed what you want to grow. If you believe the world is scary…then it is. If you believe the world is a loving place to live…then it is. Whatever you have been feeding still remains. Listen, I sometimes have to remind myself that I can finish writing this book and make sure I have it done by the deadline that is posted. Not only do I have to finish this book, but I want it to be interesting enough that you would want to buy my next one when that one comes out. My whole being wants to play words with friends on the internet, but my spirit is tugging on me to stay off the internet and Facebook until I am finished writing. That will be letting go of an

old pattern from the past. Usually I set a goal and then I start 'side tracking" and find all kinds of other jobs to do and I usually end up deciding that I am not capable. Or what's the use? As a matter of fact this week is busier than most and I believe it's because I want to get this writing done and I always believe I can fit everything in and still finish what needs to be done. I find I say yes to everything and then come up short in the long run. Once again, I am participating in people pleasing and not honoring my needs. Ok…so "letting go" is not as easy as it sounds. But when I get tired of pulling the past into the present I will definitely let go, like my grandson Carter did, when he was ready to step into the unknown. I can't wait to see what he does with the rest of his life after taking that big step forward!!!! Ok readers, on the count of three….get ready to "let go."
One….two….three...Grow!

Congratulations on your new, and prosperous life!!!

ENDINGS

Trust the process and you will be fine;
There are no accidents, it's all Divine;
Even sickness has a message to share;
It might be an opportunity to overcome fear...

Word Whisperer

Looking back on my life, I see that most everything in my life was built on endings. When you are a baby, you get to stay home for a short time before you are off to either daycare or school. And even in the school system you go to kindergarten for less than a year and then that position you take ends before you go to the next year. Each time, you build a relationship with your teacher which appears to be ongoing, because you never think ahead that it doesn't last. And it's not really your choice to move on. The system is set up a certain way and you just go with the flow. Then, you adapt, and before you know it, you are ready to graduate, and the big ending takes place. You leave school and have to find your way either into the working world, or continue to another school where the ending will take place sooner or later. Some people find a job that will be ongoing and a lot of people will go to different jobs throughout their lifetime. I know for me, I could stay at a job for just so long, and then I was on to another one. It wasn't always me leaving, because sometimes I would get asked to leave, but nevertheless, the endings were always in place for me. I believe, because of the death of my mother, at such a young age in my life, I took on the belief that the BIG things in life don't last. If I walked away, I felt more in control of the loss than having it done to me. I realize now that even in my relationships it would be me making that decision to leave. My marriage didn't stand a chance because both my husband and myself had a pattern of losing early in life, and the ending was already in place even before we got to it. People with animals experience a short time with them because the life span of most animals is short lived. For the most part, we outlive them so the painful loss will have to be experienced. Then there are movies you see and books you read and they all have endings. It doesn't take long to see a movie, and maybe a couple of days or weeks to read a book. Then it ends. The car you drive will eventually have to be replaced because it only lasts for a certain amount of time. I got involved in a church that has service Wednesday nights and Sunday mornings that I enjoyed going to. After a few years, I started getting very uncomfortable going because I realized that church doesn't end, so to speak. There is no graduation, they don't tell you to leave, and it can continue on until the day you die. My pattern of endings started surfacing and I didn't know what to do with a situation that appeared not to end. I noticed that I stopped going on Wednesdays and then Sundays started being less appealing. I started taking myself out slowly because I decided it wouldn't matter as much and the people would just get used to me being there "sometimes" until I removed myself permanently. When my car broke down, it was the perfect excuse not to go because after all, it's not my doing. It didn't matter I had a friend who could pass right by my house and give me a ride if I wanted one. I thought it was odd, after all these years of going, that I refused to have a relationship with the Pastors of the church. They represented the Spiritual Mom and Dad of the church and I just figured I had Mom and Dad issues that I never resolved fully. So needless to say I was a "hot mess" and struggling with patterns in place that would need some type of resolution. Thank God that I didn't have to figure it out because the Universe is set up to bring you lessons to help you grow so rest assured that if any of you have issues in your life, they will come to the light. My job is to just help you understand why you might be the way you are at this time so you can give yourself permission to work it out in divine timing. I would like to tell you all my issues are resolved but the truth is, there is no endings to those either. So church and issues seem to be the only things that appear to be everlasting. However, the reason I brought up the topic of endings to begin with is to remind you that at some point in your life, your endings are already in place. I am sure at one time or another you have heard "live your life, like it's your last day on earth." That is something to live by because if you do, you will get the most out of every moment, and it won't matter what ends because you will have new beginnings to take you as far as you are ready to go. I have seen people hold on to anger, unforgiveness, and resentment until it consumes them You have to be careful what you make friends with because birds of a feather.....What I am trying to say is the unseen is just as important as the seen. You don't see anger, so to speak, but you do see the reaction to anger.

Unforgiveness is hidden, but your actions speak louder than words. Resentment can show up on your face and it isn't pretty. You have to remember, if you make friends with these invisible entities, they become a part of who you are. Then the real you gets buried under all these false pretenses and once again you find yourself climbing out of a deep hole that never had to be. Celebrate an "ending" to any negative thoughts and bring in the "positive" ones because wherever you go after you end, I believe they just might come with you.

Nadia Ohar

INTUITION

When you hear without sound and you see without sight;
When you think something's wrong and you know that it's right;
There are the moments that whisper "Just Be who you are;"
Remember, you are the one that has brought you this far.....

Word Whisperer

I have now labeled myself the "Word Whisperer," therefore, I will give you my take on the word "intuition.' First of all it begins with the word "IN" which means "inner" not "outer." This is where you receive your intuitive thoughts, from the inside out, not the other way around. Then you have the word "tuition" which means "a charge for instruction." In this case we pay with our "thoughts" as the fee. You might wonder just where these thoughts come from. Some will say God, some might say the Universe and some will leave it as an inner knowingness. Because I feel a connection to God, when I ask for answers, I believe I receive them from something that is "all knowing." I believe everyone has the ability to hear the answers from the same source no matter what the label is. When the disciples wrote their messages, they got their answers from the same place we get ours today. It didn't stop there, otherwise life could not have continued and thoughts would be a waste of time. How could that be? Our lives are built on thoughts and beliefs and will be that way till the end of time. I like to think of myself as a transmitter, and the thoughts that come to me are not just for my use alone. They are to share with the world and people with the same frequencies will pick up the same thoughts as they are delivered. Other people will match their frequencies and receive what they need to hear at any given time. This is why we need to let people live their lives attuned to their own signals and not interfere with the process. How would you like to be listening to a station you enjoy, and then someone else steps in and switches the dial to whatever pleases them. And then criticizes you for liking the station that you enjoy the most. Would that truly make sense? There is nothing wrong with sharing preferences but there is something amiss when you try and call what works for you the only way to live. You got to where you are in your life by your life's lessons and everyone else will get there the same way. After all, this world is structured for us to live and learn by playing the game. Even in the game of football, if there is "pass interference,' that could cost someone the game. So it's important to know when to share your viewpoints or wait for someone to ask, because then you know they are ready to hear what you have to say. Sometimes it looks like we can get answers from books, but that is only because you are looking for that answer from the book, and only you know whether that answer will work for you. It's not about how many people agree with you or disagree with you. If you were the only person that preferred something a certain way and twenty others went another way, it doesn't mean there is something wrong with you. As long as you are not harming another, you have that right! Again, numbers don't make people more right than others!!!Okay, having said that, let's get back to intuition and what that looks like on a regular basis. Sometimes a thought comes to us out of the blue, like thinking about another person, and the next thing you know, you run into them shortly thereafter, or you get a call from them. When you send energy out there it has to go somewhere. If a name is attached to that thought, I believe the other person receives a signal from you, and the connection is made invisible at first and then into the visible. When you meditate on a certain subject or question, it's the same type of scenario. You are sending out thoughts and they are connecting to the right source, and then they come back to you in the form of an answer. In some cases the answer lies dormant within you and when you are ready to know, the answer will surface after you clear out all the deceptions you put in place for your own protection. Sometimes, when I resist the truth, I can feel my body tense and consequently, I block the flow either by focusing on something else to avoid hearing what I don't want to hear, or I involve myself in something that makes me feel good at that time, like a dessert, movie, or computer chat. Now, I am more open to the truth, so my need to avoid is less. I focus on keeping the invisible channel where my thoughts flow through, purified and unclogged. I do this by participating in prayer, affirmations, and using only good thoughts throughout the day. If a negative thought gets through, I just dismiss it and let it go. I don't give it extra attention because that would help it grow and I need room for thoughts that benefit my life and the lives of others. The "flow" is the place where your abundance comes to you, as well as loving relationships, and health and well-being. You can't let something in if there is junk piled up at the place of entry. The way you can do this is decide how you want to start your day. Do you want to start it with a peaceful meditation, song, or conversation with a good friend? Any way you start, you will finish the same way. Be careful of using statements, like "I'm having a bad day." The day is long and you might have some inconvenience during the day, but that doesn't constitute the whole day! When you call it a "bad day" you negate any of the good that might have been there. Don't keep that channel clogged with negative thinking! Keep that pathway open to all good things! When I wrote my first book titled "Peace in the Jungle," I was all excited because I felt that it was a best seller and I just knew that people would be drawn to that type of book which contained the drama and misfortunes of people's lives and the underlying deception that sparked murder and malicious acts of hurtful behavior. Oh yes, it was the kind of drama that could excite anyone. But then, my intuition kicked in, and I started receiving messages that I didn't quite want to hear. I was hearing that it was not to my advantage to fill people's minds with that kind of information, and that whatever I put out there can somehow come back into my life. I was even shown, the kind of energy that was associated with those kinds of books. I won't mention any names but I became aware of the addictive behavior of a few people who had a couple of books that were questionable on their book shelves. I know I was being shown this because I had a choice to make. I could either ignore my intuition and take a chance that I was "misinformed" or I could trust that I was being shown a better way and decide what kind of information I would feed to other people. This was a decision I had to make almost 25 years ago. I did listen and I did destroy those writings and let me tell you, it was one of the hardest things I had to do. Now as I sit writing this book, it might not be as exciting as the other one, but I will say this, it feels good to tell the truth. I don't mind filling conscious minds with information that could benefit many people who are ready to hear what needs to be said. These thoughts don't belong to me anymore than children belong to parents. Like it or not, you have them for a short time before you have to let them go to find a home of their own.

WORD ASSOCIATION

A beLIEf doesn't always make is so;
It's just something you think you know;
If there happens to be an opposing view;
Their story is made of thoughts like you...

Word Whisperer

I thought it might be fun to play a little game of word association and then put the words to a story and find out more about yourself. Here's how it works. I will give you a list of words and you will write down the first word that comes to your mind. Get a separate piece of paper and write your answers. Then you will fill in the blanks with the words you came up with in the right sequence and see if it says something about you. Sometimes it makes sense and other times it might not, but either way it is a chance to have some fun. Okay, here is your list. Don't think too long and hard. Write the 1st word that come to mind. There are no right and wrong answers.

1. Father	8. Vacation	15. Waterfall
2. Mother	9. Happy	16. Weather
3. Love	10. Baby	17. Car
4. Kiss	11. Friend	18. Music
5. Food	12. War	19. Death
6. Movie	13. Alone	20. Home
7. Book	14. Pain	

Next, fill in the blanks to the story below, using the words you wrote, in order, and then read the story back to yourself using the words you associated with each word. Have fun!

My _____ heart helps me when I _____ my inner child because I know that _____ and the _____ feeling I get when I think I am _____. The memories are still fresh in my _____thoughts and I only think of the _____when I am alone or afraid. I like to go to _____ where I can be _____because I can reflect on _____images and the good times I had in my _____ life. I feel the _____when I am rejected or abandoned but I realize it's because I am _____. The _____ I feel is overwhelming until I close my eyes and allow the _____to soothe my soul. I look forward to the _____days and take my _____away from the _____of the world. The _____that I felt is no longer with me and I find solace in my thoughts of _____.

I do hope that was fun and you can even try it on your friends. You will discover that people have different associations with each word. This is why you cannot judge what everyone else is thinking or how they should match your way of thinking. It's hard to believe that one word can have so many different word associations. Even the dictionary will give you a meaning to suit everyone, but even with that, thoughts are not all the same. I have a friend who loves to go north when she goes on vacation in the cold region of the world. I cannot believe that she wouldn't prefer to go south where the days are warm and the beaches are inviting. But this is just another case of someone else preferring to do it different from what I would expect. This brings me to the topic of "expectations." Sometimes it doesn't serve you to expect an outcome to be a certain way because you can set yourself up for disappointment. On the other hand, it's been said that "you get what you expect" so it can get very confusing. When we set our sights on having what we want and expect it to manifest the way we think it should, we might be limiting the way we receive the outcome we want. The Universe might have something "better," so to speak, for our highest good, so we don't want to put limits on our expectations. I believe the disappointments come when we set our sights way too high, and then expect something to happen that doesn't really match reality. I might want to make a million dollars this year, but I might be working at a place that pays me $10.00 an hour and if I'm unwilling to change my reality by finding another way to increase my finances, then my thoughts will not be in alignment with reality. You can change your reality using your thoughts, but your thoughts will have to be truthful. You can call things that be not as though they were, but that too, has to be in alignment with your lifestyle and your belief system. You don't have to know how the outcome will take place. You just have to believe that it will take place. I can visualize a new car and put a picture of it in front of me to keep my thoughts focused on my outcome, but my thoughts have to have something to work with in order to manifest the car I want. I'm not saying it's not possible to receive something big in your life that you did not expect, but I will say this, on some level, your subconscious helped to create your end result without you being conscious of your thought process. Your subconscious plays a big part in your life and when you practice conscious living, you just bring that subconscious mind to the forefront and work together as one mind. That's why it is so important to pay attention to your outer world so you know what is going on in the "inner" world. It can also be fun to set a goal, work with it in the invisible realm, be thankful for it before you get it, and then watch it manifest into your life so you can have testimony the way it works. You can encourage others to use the same methods to help them with their goals. There is nothing like a good testimony, which is a form of evidence that your thoughts can work for you. Just make sure you are plugged into your source and there is nothing you can't accomplish when you put your mind to it! Another fun thing to do is if you listen to music, set your mind to hearing what the second or third song played has to say to you personally. You have to pick which sequence is going to be for you, before you hear the song, and then watch how cleverly the Universe works with giving you what you need to hear. Decide if it's going to be every second song or every third song but whatever you decide, be ready for unexpected results. I even have fun with using a self-help book and asking God to give me a message that I need to hear and then I open to a certain page and there it is! Just what I needed to hear! There are many ways to find out what messages are in store for you. Be creative and then be open to receive. It's just that simple! You can even do it with this book. Ask a question or decide what page you open to and then point to a paragraph with your eyes closed and there will be information just for you.

TIME

T"I""me" is of the essence, it contains "I" and "me;"
Without the use of time, we could never be;
There is always enough and it's oh so free;
If time's not the issue, then it must be me.....

Word Whisperer

It's funny but I hear so many people say they don't have enough time for this or they don't have time for that. What exactly is this word called time? I did notice that the word "time" has the word "me" at the end of it so I would like to think that time has something to do with "me." Does time remain invisible so that it cannot be manipulated by my demands? When we think of God we hear that he always was and will always be. That means no beginning and no end which is probably a good way to define "time." There really is no substance to time other than an image of a clock or a watch that tells you what time it is. You have to trust that the minutes and hours are just a way to reveal time in a way that you can understand it. Now if we break time into 24 hour intervals then I have to believe we all start with the same amount of time in a day. No one is given more and no one is given less. So what it really boils down to is how do we use the time that is allotted to us in this lifetime? Do we waste time? Do we see time as a valuable commodity? Do we age according to our belief in time gone by? We do use the concept of time in various ways but we will never be able to look time directly in the eye because there is no time to see. Time is made up so that we can have a sense of order in our world system. So why do we put so much energy on something that doesn't appear to be real? Once again, it's our thoughts that determine our reality, not necessarily the thing of itself. I know, for me, I would complain that I didn't have enough time to do this or finish that, but the real truth was I wasn't using my time wisely. I would prioritize my day, but then I would side track or get involved in something else that would pull me away from my goal. I also look at time as I would look at money in my pocket. How do I spend my money? How do I spend my time?

Both valuable commodities, but possibly misused in the process. Money only has the value I place on it and that is the same concept regarding time. I might complain there is not enough of either one, but I have a part in deciding to go without by keeping my false beliefs in place. How do I untwist what is already in place? It might not be that complicated. I just start putting the pieces together, in this case truth, and then the puzzle becomes clearer as it forms into an image that I can fully understand. I am totally fascinated with how we can take time and make it into day light savings time and then switch it back when the time is right. I mean, we are not really changing anything but just assigning new meaning to the day. It was always fascinating to me how we set our time to one world clock and everyone always seems in sync with the right time even though we have clocks with batteries that seem to wear down and keep track of time at a slower pace at times. But even with that, we all make it to work on time because ironically we all seem to match. It doesn't seem possible to me because there are so many people in the world that have to be in sync with the same time we work with and it all seems to work. I really don't know why I felt the need to talk about time, but for some reason, it came to my mind and I do want to continue to talk about the mind and the thoughts that follow. I will say that the word "time" is used in many conversations. "What time is it?" "It's time to go." "I don't have time right now." Because you always have time because time never leaves you, but it is just another concept of how we use our thoughts. For something that is really nothing, it is used quite a bit in people's lives. I think it's important to remember the next time we use the word time, we are really talking about something that doesn't exist, as such, but something we labeled and think we get use of it in different ways. The only reason I bring this up is because I want you to understand how the mind really works.

Now it's time for me to move on to my next subject…..

THINK CALLED EARTH

"There's a peaceful way to end strife;
It's called an appreciation of all life;
Hidden agendas must come to the light;
To dissolve mankind's need to fight....

Word Whisperer

Okay, the Word Whisperer is at it again. I look at the word "earth" and right away I see the word "ear" which lets me know this planet is set up to "hear" what you have to say. Words need to be spoken in order to hear them and this world is made up of thoughts, words, and then people. It has even been said that this world was "spoken" into being. "Let there be light" and then there was. The words are spoken first, and then the manifestation next. When I first typed the title to this chapter, I intended to write "This thing called Earth" but unintentionally I typed the word "think" instead and decided to leave it that way. I mean "thoughts" derived from "think" seems to be a constant theme running through this book so I left it that way. It fascinates me that this giant ball floating in the Universe is a big part of our own life. How often do we take time to see the miracle in living on this big planet or to see this planet as a miracle? I mean we celebrate each other at least once a year with a birthday but what do we do for our planet? We take it for granted, maybe in the same way we took our hard working parents for granted because they were just there for our needs and didn't ask a whole lot in return. Well this chapter is dedicated to our planet and I am sending love and gratitude for allowing all of us to reside and experience a portion of our lives in so many different ways. It feels so good to understand what this planet stands for and the miraculous manifestations that are allowed to take place because we are all given so many opportunities to produce anything that our hearts desire. The planet is what I see as "unconditional" and never interferes with our choices and it is now important for me to give back to something that has given me so much without physically asking for anything in return. I know we can all do our part if we just know what to do. I looked online to see if there were a few tips I could pass on so we could start making a difference right away. Buy Energy Star appliances the next time you are in the market to buy another appliance. Replace your light bulbs with compact fluorescent lights and make sure you turn them off when you leave the room, shop at thrift stores and buy used or refurbished products, create an organic vegetable garden, drive a more fuel efficient car, walk, bike or car pool when you can, use a reusable water bottle, recycle paper, glass and plastics, turn your computer off at night instead of leaving it in sleep mode, choose matches over lighters, use rechargeable batteries, pay your bill online and I am sure you can think of a dozen or more ways in which to honor the planet that gives you life. This planet Earth is really a fascinating feature. I like to look at everything in 3-D mode and when I step back and look at our Earth, I see that it is in the shape of a circle. The circle of life with no beginning and no end, but a continuation of more of the same, but used in a different way. A circle is a circle is a circle, and it doesn't matter who the artist is, the circle stays the same. And that's how I see our planet as staying the same, but with different happenings that match different individual experiences but still remaining intact and available to all. This is why I am proud to say that I am an "Earthican" and will do my part in celebrating this amazing planet. See where thoughts will take you. I really never thought much about the planet and now I can even participate in keeping it energy efficient. I look at the planet as one big giant book and we are all creating our own stories and each one of us is just a chapter in the whole scheme of things. Can you imagine a book of that size? Come on, use your thoughts and let your imagination take you to a place you wouldn't ordinarily go. What story do you want to add to this magnificent book? It is choice if you want your life to be a mystery, comedy, thriller, or love story or maybe a little of it all. You're the author so have at it! In closing I want to thank planet Earth again on behalf of all of us. It will be a pleasure serving this planet for a change!

THE PATH

"If someone wants to walk in your shoes, make sure you take your feet out first."

Word Whisperer

When I first created "The Path" for others to walk and listen to guided messages along the way, my intention was to create a board game at first. I wanted to create something that was fun and people would be able to go back to the old fashioned way of living and playing games at the table. Then, what I really wanted to create was to have the person be the pawn instead of using a pawn to move on the board. I wanted the person using the path to be able to participate fully in walking the path and then they would draw from the "Path Cards." Now, I had to meditate and get the proper messages to create the "Path Cards" because I believe, once again, that the Universe knows what we need to hear, say and do. So, with pen in hand, I started writing messages on paper that flowed through my mind and was so grateful to be used as a channel for this information. Not only was I instructed to make 'path cards" but I was inspired to create cards with "Words of Wisdom," "Forgiveness cards" and "Affirmations." So in this chapter, we are all going to walk "The Path" and find out what your source wants you to know. I will start by taking five minutes to get quiet and invite all the angelic messengers and guides to lead us to our highest good. I thank God in advance for setting up this divine encounter and I am truly blessed to be an instrument in this divine process. The first Path Card states: "Be aware of the "addictions" that seem to control your life. You are in control of whatever you put into your body. "Substance" has to be chosen. It doesn't choose you! Choose an "Affirmation" and move ahead one space. ...Affirmation: "Love is the essence of who I am. I reflect this love in my life by seeing the Divine in all whom I come in contact with. Love is always at the forefront even in times of trouble or discord. I am quick to resolve issues in the name of love. All is well." Let that set in for a moment before we move on. Next... the path card says: "It's time to receive

what God wants you to have. Pick a "forgiveness card" and listen to the message to make room for what He has for you". Here is what the "forgiveness card says: "I trust the process of life and hold nothing against any person that has crossed my path. I do realize that anything that takes place in my life is necessary and helps me grow. The journey may seem painful at times but I know in the long run, it's for my highest good!" Let that set in. Another path card...."When you worry, you invite those thoughts into your mind so that you can remain fearful and stressed. Quickly replace "worry thoughts" with positive thoughts such as "I trust the process of life" and then relax. Your life will always reflect the thoughts you are thinking." ....Next ....as we move forward....."It's time to "let go" of the familiar and take a chance on something new! YOU CAN DO IT!" This message is for someone who is holding back taking that next step into your destiny. You have a whole cheering squad that you don't even know about...people who have gone before you are rooting for you to succeed. Don't let missed opportunities get in the way of sabotaging what God has in store for you! Your next path card tells you that "Sickness is not an option. Do not make room for any dis-ease in your life. You wouldn't allow a stranger into your home so don't allow anything into your body that you don't invite in. An affirmation will strengthen your quest to stay healthy." Here is your affirmation: "I make time to pray and meditate on answers to some of my questions that need careful consideration. I trust and have faith in the goodness of life and eliminate any fears that might hold me back. I am truly blessed." ....Okay, don't get tired...we need to keep moving forward. The next path card is "When you were growing up as a child, do you remember your parent's words about money? Do those thoughts hold true for you today? Are there any thoughts you would like to change so you can have what you say you want in life?" Take some time to answer those questions because we are not in a rush and it's important to confront certain things along the way so you can make room for more. Deep breathe...ok next card! "When is the last time you put yourself first?" .....If it takes you longer than thirty seconds to answer it has been way too long. If not, keep on loving yourself the way God loves you every minute of the day!" Get ready to hear more.....
Okay..... "Any time you are worried about what someone else

might think, you have stepped out of your life and into theirs. If God had a blessing for you at that moment you would not be there and you would miss out on your blessing. This is a serious reminder for you to stay in your life and allow others to be as they are." I think that is self-explanatory...you know who you are.....We are going to keep going on this special, spiritual path adventure. "Someone has a partner who is holding on to the past. He takes two steps forward and one step back. You do the same because his behavior affects you. When you are done with this dance, you will be able to move forward. Otherwise you will stay where you are and miss opportunities that are one step away." Wow... Someone has to take the lead and if someone keeps pulling you back, you might have to go on without that person and they just might follow you! Okay....we have to keep moving forward. "Something has been troubling you lately. Just know that God is in charge and hears your pleas for help. This problem is being resolved right now!!! It's time to pick a forgiveness card and release all fear! Forgiveness: "I forgive myself for the foolish choices I made that not only hurt me, but hurt others, as well. I forgive myself for the need to be "right' that overshadowed the need to be "loved." I forgive myself for the lies I told to justify my behavior in order to continue "being right." I now move on in a loving and caring manner." Isn't forgiveness sweet? Makes you feel warm all over.....Are you all ready to keep moving forward? Here we go! Another message...."Just remember, the discomfort you feel in your relationship is propelling you forward to a deeper level of intimacy. Don't turn back, but rather ask God for the support you need. You will be presented with an "affirmation" to help you in your growth." Affirmation: "I know in order to truly love myself, I need to forgive myself and others for any and all imperfections that created pain in my life. I allow myself to "let go" of expectations and accept myself at all levels." You know, sometimes we just need to realize that there is no such thing as perfect unless you are talking about God, spirit, or the divine. This is why we have to give ourselves permission to make "mistakes" along the way so you can allow others that same grace. If you can't do it for yourself, than you can't do it for others......next path card...."Someone still needs your forgiveness. Close your eyes and mentally forgive this person!" We cannot move on until this is handled… another forgiveness card might help. ""I forgive myself for holding on to "Self Pity" as a way to depend on others. I realize the pain I experienced along the way was just a tool to help me grow in the areas I most wanted to keep hidden. I let go of the old patterns that no longer serve me and allow the goodness go flow into my life. There is nothing to regret for everything has its purpose….."Take a deep breath….and then let it out before we continue. Let each message sink in, for it is here to help you….. Okay…next…."God wants you to be well. Why go against His wishes for your life? Your relationship with Him is ultimately your relationship with self. Love your God with all your heart and you will want to do what's best for you. Read another "forgiveness card" in order to make room for "unconditional love." Here it is: "I forgive myself for all the times I put God second in my life and tried to participate in the "worldly system" which did not work. I am sorry for all the opportunities I passed up because I was invested in being afraid. I thank God for a second chance to put Him first in my life!" Some of you are being sent these messages for a reason. There are no accidents if you are participating in this Spiritual Journey because you are hearing these "specialized' messages that need to be heard. I am just the messenger so I am going to keep going until we are at the end of this path. Next…"There is no glory in being a martyr…yes, we know, you want to be the hero. You will be the one who goes without so someone else is okay. You're self-sacrificing…but just remember, most pity parties are celebrated alone!!! Wow. Even I needed to hear that one. That was always a big part of my life, trying to be everyone's hero but nothing left for myself. You will very seldom see a "happy" martyr and for that reason alone, should make you conscious of the fact that you don't want to do that anymore. And believe it or not, the person you are sacrificing for is going to be just fine with or without you!!!! Okay. Onward…we just have a little ways to go before we are finished walking our path. Next…"A battle goes on inside of you. It's between two monsters. One is evil. It is anger, greed, arrogance, self-pity, guilt, resentment, inferiority, lies, false pride, superiority and ego. The other is good. It is joy, peace, love, hope, serenity, humility, kindness, sympathy, generosity, truth, compassion and faith. Which monster will win? The one you feed of course! That was always a favorite of mine. And how true that is because what we give energy to grows. I'm sure we talked about that in previous chapters. Are you ready to move on? Come on…just a little more. Ok...here's something for you. "There can be no happiness if the things you do, don't line up with the things you believe in. Get clear on what's true for you and go for it!!!"That makes perfect sense. Do you ever find you think one thing and the next thing you know you are doing something else that is really not in alignment? With your intention? I know for me, I think I can make some things work that are just not workable. It takes longer than it needs to be if I would just stay with the truth of who I am…Okay…… Next…"You are now releasing old patterns that no longer serve you. Pick a "Wisdom Card" to support you in your growth. Thank God for the change that is taking place in your life right now." "On a scale from 1-10, how grateful are you for your life? Remember, if you choose 10, you have to be grateful for EVERYTHING. Even the hard times because those are the situations that nudge or push you into your place of having more…." If you picked a number less than 10, decide why you would settle for less when the 10 is possible. ….One more step and we have completed that part of our spiritual journey. "Do you realize "letting go" of something that has served its purpose actually makes room for God to add more into your life…Something that will serve you now! Can you think of something you might need to "let go" of in your life at this time? After you answer this question, mentally let go of this person or thing by saying good bye once and for all, and thank it for being in your life because it did help you grow. The "letting go" will help you even more……Congratulations on walking your path. You had a chance to "sample" what it would be like to hear different messages from the Universe about your life and actually deal with some of the issues that come up along the way. This particular path had a theme of "forgiveness" on route as well as opportunities to confront some of the issues in your life. I do take appointments for this "Spiritual Path Adventure" so you can pick your path and then walk it. Rest assured, that anything that you need to hear, will present itself. No two paths are the same, and you leave here knowing you were spoken to from the place of the Divine. Thanks for your participation and I hope you had fun in the process.

EXCUSES AND JUSTIFICATIONS

Life is a mirror and you are the reflection;
The image that shows is not fooled by deception;
Just because you paint over the image that's there;
Remember your true colors will always appear...

Word Whisperer

Did you ever notice that just about anyone can justify their actions regardless of how foolish their choices may look after they made that choice? It is amazing how the human mind works. We can take ourselves so far out of reality that even our excuses sound wonderful! I mean, you have to admit, the mind is a terrible thing to waste so why not open it up to all the creative ways your stories can help to keep you right where you are, without moving ahead. Isn't that the place of comfort and familiarity? Why is it that some of us want to keep the same movie rolling over and over again when a new one is available anytime we are willing to leave the theater, so to speak. That's right. It just takes stepping out of the old story and creating a new story. The old story is the one in the past. Now, I am guessing that some of you watch some of the old movies on television and you see that there is quite a difference from those and the movies of the now. You see, that there is some improvement with quality and special effects and other things. Why would you want to get stuck in the past when the present is so much more interesting and creative? But that is exactly what people do. You hear about people talking about the good old days and really believe that the time back there was the best. But truthfully, in time, things do improve. Otherwise, nothing would change and we would keep everything the same. But the truth is, everything in life is motion and we are moving and changing a little at a time. Even if you were to cling to the past, everything around you is changing anyway, so you would have to match your surroundings eventually, like it or not. My need to mention all this is to encourage you to "catch up" to the now, and drop your justifications and old stories and embrace the new. Don't let fear try to hold you back, because fear belongs in the past, not in the present moments. Fear was brought into your life in the past to help you make choices that would hold you back so you could feel secure and protected by staying stagnant and not advancing into the unknown. That's right. Fear was used as an insecure friend and you teamed up in the past. However, when you let go of "fear" it finds another home with someone who is willing to stay in the box. You, however, are ready for the present and the new adventure that awaits you!

I do remember living in the box and every once in a while I would pop my head out and realize there was so much more out there and how many of you know that once you know, you can't go back? And if you do, you can't stay anymore. I had every excuse in the book why I could not do something. I used money as an excuse, I used time as an excuse, I used the kids as an excuse, whatever it was, I had it covered with excuses. What happens when you get rid of the stories and excuses?

You are left with the truth. You can do anything if you are willing to do what it takes. I didn't want to know whether I could do it because I would have to take responsibility for my life and then decide, not let something decide for me. There is something to be said about taking responsibility for your life and not blaming an outside source because you can take yourself as far as you want to go and its' not really about something else…it's about you! Believe it or not that is the good news! When you are confronted with a decision to make and are encompassed in fear, the first thing you can ask yourself is "What is the worst that could happen if I decide to move forward with this?" You will probably find out it's not as scary as you think when you come up with that answer. Remove that barrier in place that stops you right from the "get go." I challenge you to take one day out of your life and simply remove your story and excuses on anything that surfaces that day. If you decide not to do something, do not follow your decision with a story. Leave it at "no." Most people who want to feel right about something are always defending their position when a simple yes or no would be sufficient. That takes a lot of energy to attach a story to everything you do. You don't have to live like your life is playing out in a courtroom. Then there is the other extreme where someone might live their life like they don't have a say at all. You know, the ones who are never certain about anything. They stay vague in their responses and give you "I don't know" and "I'm not sure" and "maybe" when it comes to making a decision. They don't even bother coming up with a story because their story is clear from the get go. You know, "it doesn't matter to me" because they will never put themselves in a position to be blamed for anything. So making no decision means they can't be wrong, but the truth is, they can't be right either. Their life is built on everyone else making it okay for them. They gave up their power a long time ago and decided to stay "unplugged." That is such a waste of life. It reminds me of a gift that you refuse to unwrap and see what is inside. It's like having a car but refusing to drive it. And on some level, it is insulting to give someone a gift and then they put it aside like it's meaningless. Life is a gift to use and not to ignore like it has no value. I absolutely can relate to this type of living. I put myself in a position where everyone else knew better than me about what I should and should not do and consequently gave up thinking for myself. Then, I would end up rebelling against others, because after all, I had to surface somehow in the whole scheme of things. No surprise my life was full of extremes. But that was the past, and we all have to let go of a past before we can participate fully in the present. The future is taken care of because it has everything to do with the present. I would suggest starting with the "little things." Get in the driver's seat and make small decisions about the place to go. Stop letting everyone else decide for you and when you make a decision, don't let someone take it away like it has no value. Eventually, you might draw in more people who respect what you have to say, and give you the space to be who you are. Your life will start changing when you make the "shift" even in small matters. No one builds a house with no foundation if they want it to stand firm in the hard times. And that is what you are doing when you start by making small decisions. You are laying the foundation for bigger decisions as they arise. Make a small goal because when you look at saving a thousand dollars you might just say I can't do that but you can take a small amount every week, even if it's five dollars, and it will add up to that thousand dollars that you thought you couldn't do. Start small and stop looking at the end result which appears bigger than you can handle. That is self-defeating behavior and you won't get anywhere by spinning the wheels on your vehicle. If you go to a restaurant and you ask for something and they bring it to you, but it's not the way you want it, you need to send it back in a nice way, and get what you want. This is a way of developing that muscle of knowing you can have what you say you want. I always like to look at the "spiritual side" of life and realize that I am the vehicle for the spirit that chose me to carry it through this lifetime. How sad would it be if I just lived in a limited way, when the limitless spirit is ready for a great adventure! It's like having a baby and never leaving the house so the baby doesn't get the benefit of experiencing the vast and wondrous world. So as a reminder, don't be afraid to make decisions, and if you feel fear, do it anyway! You are the captain of your voyage and the captain does not hand over the wheel to its passengers. Be all of who you are! I can't tell you how excited I am to be in this position to encourage anyone who needs to hear these words. I so needed to hear this when I was emerging into who I am today and let me tell you, it is so worth making the changes that will benefit your life to the fullest! I do want to add that these changes are not changing who you are because the truth is you are already perfect, whole, and complete. The changes and choices you make are just a reflection of where you want to take yourself and how far you want to go. A swimming pool is always a swimming pool, but there are certain levels and depth to it, that can be used if you so choose. It doesn't change the swimming pool being a pool, but again, there are levels and depth to it. Just like us. We are who we are, and there are levels we can take ourselves to if we so choose. It's funny, but what comes to mind when I think of the world we live in at this time, is technology. To some people, it is such a natural process to participate in this system. To others, they don't participate in all the latest technology gadgets and don't feel they are really missing out on anything big. This is because, as I said before, we are all perfect, whole and complete. Technology is just another level you can participate in, but it doesn't make you any more of a person than you are already are. So start by celebrating the real you and make decisions according to your needs. And always remember, YOU CAN!!!!!

ARE YOU A MATCH?

Sometimes you need to be your own best friend
Especially when your heart is on the mend;
Who else would know you better than you?
You are strong enough to make it through......

Word Whisperer

I thought it might be fun to make another list and you can give one to a friend and keep one for yourself. It will be fun to compare your answers to your friend's answers and see just how compatible you really are.

On a scale from 1 to 10, how happy are you?

Is it more important to have money or love in your life? Pick one.

Name an important goal in your life right now.

What would you pick? Steak or Lobster?

What movie would you choose...mystery, romance or documentary?

Do you believe in God?

How much money would be enough for you?

Say something about your Mother in one word.

Describe you Dad in one word

What do you think is your best quality?

Compare your answers and see how many match the other person's answers. Don't judge or be critical because there are no wrong answers. It's just fun to see if you all think alike. And if not, you get to learn something about the other person. And that's what we are all about. Learning and emerging! I do think, in some cases, it is important to match on some of the bigger issues because there is strength in numbers and a house divided will fall. Just keep in mind, in the process, that you are not more right than others with the answers you choose. Answers are just ways to reveal where we are at this time in our lives. If someone is at the store after you have already been there, it doesn't mean their timing is off. It just means that they go according to their own divine timing. I always felt that way when people would show up at a certain time, whether it be work, or maybe an event, and they would apologize profusely for being late, but I don't believe in "late" or "early." I believe in "divine timing." You are where you are supposed to be at all times. Now maybe you would want to debate that because there are statements like "being at the wrong place at the wrong time", but even with that, I would venture to say that there is a beneficial lesson in something that is going to take place exactly where you decided to end up. Now are all lessons sugar and spice? Of course not! Most lessons reek of pain and sorrow but unfortunately this is how we grow in the process. I have said it before and I will say it again, a seed has to push its way through a mound of dirt in order to blossom in the sun. You might want to write that one down so you will have it for reference when it feels like you are going through a hard time. I like to post all kinds of affirmations around the house and when I am done with those, I put up some new ones. Ultimately, they do come in handy when I am going through something that feels uncomfortable. My son recently was feeling sick, and I felt helpless because I couldn't do anything to make him feel better and I had to find some way to feel better about the situation. I have my own private prayer line which is connected to Silent Unity, which has been so helpful in pulling me out of "worry" and "concern." I love hearing the other person on the other line telling me that they join together with me for Kevin's perfect health. When God, the source of life, is brought into the mix, it instantly brings a veil of peace over me, as we affirm with assurance that every cell and tissue is being renewed. This is where faith and belief connect and join together for our highest good. I have come a long way from where I used to be. I can't tell you the number of times I would cry at the drop of a hat, or worry about everything that could happen if I couldn't be there to fix it. I didn't label myself as a worrier, I thought I was just being a realist about everything, but now I know the difference between being real and creating negative energy around my experiences. I never knew at one time, my thoughts even carried energy with them. I didn't know that I created situations in my life by the way I thought and acted. I think I was afraid to take control over my life so, for me, it was easier to believe a lie than to live in truth. It wasn't until I was ready for the truth, that I drew in the people I needed to hear, and the books I needed to read for the growth that needed to take place. I am so grateful today for listening and putting into action the goals I have set in place for myself. My goal is to create a loving, intimate relationship with someone who loves me unconditionally and live in a two bedroom house by the water and appreciate warm, sunny days. I would also like to welcome clients into my home for spiritual sessions that will encourage them to live a purposeful life that they came here to live. They will be sent home with "spiritual tools" that they can use for a foundation for higher living. I am so blessed that I can share my gifts and inner wisdom to others who already know what I have to say. They are just looking for confirmation for what they already know.

YOU CAN PLEASE SOME OF THE PEOPLE......

SOME OF THE TIME......

Sometimes saying nothing speaks louder than saying something....

Word Whisperer

Okay...this is for all you "people pleasers" out there who think you can make everyone happy and then hyperventilate when you find out someone was not happy with you or your performance. Come on. It has probably happened to everyone on this planet one time or another. I know for me, growing up I was taught to act a certain way around people and say the right words, you know, the words that would please others, not necessarily the truth, but what did that matter. As long as the other person felt good, it implied you did a good thing. It didn't matter you were chipping away at your beliefs and putting everyone else first. It just mattered that the other person was happy and pleased with you. This pattern of people pleasing carried into my adult life where I would be on automatic pilot when it came to giving to others. It didn't matter if I was too tired and wanted to say no to some of the requests that came my way; it just mattered that I would give to the other person and ignore my own needs. I wanted the other person to make it okay for me, but it never happened that way. They want what they want and if you are willing to give it to them, why would they be the ones to say no? So ultimately it fell on me to make my life better and go through the experience of someone being disappointed or feeling bad. Wow! That was harsh! I mean, seeing someone feeling bad and not doing anything to make it better. It's called dependency withdrawal and that can take some time to clear out before you are actually clean and sober, so to speak. I didn't realize how addicted I was to making the other person happy until I wore myself down and had to say no when a situation arose that I just could not do. I had to live with the other person being mad at me. What I learned was, I didn't die in the process, and I was able to give more to myself when I wasn't giving

141

it all away to everyone else. If there was something I liked and someone else liked it too, I would automatically say "you take it!" I conditioned myself to not really care about anything because I wouldn't claim it for myself and "ownership" was a thing of the past. How do you balance out these type of relationships where you are the doer and they are the taker? First of all, I believe you have to be honest and decide how much doing you really want to do. You have to get honest with your own needs and you have to be honest when you don't want to do something for someone else. They will find someone else to do it instead. You have to get over your abandonment issues and realize you are never alone even if every person in your life decided to walk away from you. You are enough! You don't have to get your needs met by all the people in your life either. Balance has to come into the mix and boundaries have to be honored. The give and take has to be both ways, and you have to be willing to let go of "one way" relationships. You might have felt like you were in control and that's why you stay in those type of relationships but sooner or later you will get tired of doing and going without. The price you pay is not worth holding on to those types of relationships. Even a dog is happy with a pat on the head, and you are much more than that. You have to go back to a time where you felt loved and appreciated for who you are, the beautiful, loving, caring, child of God, all deserving of all good things. Meditate on who you are and let that love in. It starts with "self-love" and you can provide that for yourself. The benefits of loving yourself are amazing! You will never allow yourself to be treated the way you have in the past and you will draw in people who care about you the way you care about yourself. Don't let other people's needs over ride what you need for yourself. If you do, you will be in the same boat; taking and not able to give. I do recommend taking time once a day to give yourself something that you would appreciate and be thankful for. It can be a good meal that is nutritious, a walk in the park, a trip to the hairdressers, or simply meditating on all the good things in your life. Remember to fill your mind with words of love because someone else may guess what you need to hear, but ultimately you know what you need and you don't have to wait for someone else to give that to you. And really, when you are being all that you are, you are actually people pleasing in a good way! People will enjoy being around you more because happiness is contagious and happiness is created out of love.

Nadia Ohar

RELATIONSHIPS

RelationSHIPS are like the waves of an ocean;
They seldom stay calm and are always in motion;
They take you to places you have never been;
That's when you know your ship has come in...

Word Whisperer

The word "relationship" starts with the prefix "re" which means "again" because one thing is for sure, we get to do relationships over and over again. It ends with the word "ship" which can constitute anything from "two ships in the night" to wondering which person is "captain of the ship" or possibly a cruise ship honeymoon. That's what my role as a "Word Whisperer" is, to take the words to their fullest meaning. I do see the letter "I" in the middle of the word, because you matter, but nowhere do I see the word "me," which has a tendency to pull you away from working together. There is the word elation" which means exaltation, which means to elevate to a higher level. If you are in the right relationship you will participate in helping each other to elevate to the next level. In other words, you will encourage with words from your mouth, over and over again, and never tear down the other person because lasting relationships are built on trust and transformation. Abuse in a relationship usually stems from the need to control and dominate another person because they felt powerless in their life, and now they get out of balance with the power they use to get their way without compassion or understanding of the other person. Self-centered needs are usually demanded instead of earned in the relationships. If you are in a healthy relationship you will get your turn. Most of us bring only what we know to the table and that is usually how we were treated growing up in our households. I know for me, there was fighting and hollering in my house and that's how I would communicate in my relationships. Usually, relationships of this sort don't work and when you are done blaming the other partner and ready to take responsibility for your part in the break up, you can feel the loss and move on to the next one. If you don't spend time alone before you get into another relationship, you will have the same outcome because you are "replacing" that person with someone else and that won't work. You are just putting the loss that you need to experience fully, on hold, and it will have to be released through another form or another relationship. Either way, you cannot escape feeling the loss you pretend that you didn't have. It's in place and now you have no choice because truth always comes to the light. Some people drink to avoid, and some people even become workaholics, but the truth is, you will find some time to be alone with yourself, because you can run but you can't hide. They say that if you are a girl, you marry your father, and if you are a boy, you marry your mother. If this is true, then I would find out before I start dating someone, how they felt about their mother or father to begin with. You can save yourself a lot of grief if you do this first. I would also recommend that you heal the relationship you have with your parents so you are able to get into a healthy relationship and not just one that you have to work out mother/father issues. However you choose to do it, it will be done. I believe some people take on a relationship with God to practice loving and practice being loved. It is safer to do it this way, because on some level, you are still in control of what you let in and you get to practice what it's like to care about something that is supposed to care about you. You are not going to be fighting with God so that eliminates one negative out of your relationship. Practice makes perfect so it's a safe way to learn how to love unconditionally. We do have relationships with everything in our life. Our homes, our money, our cars are also built on relationships. How do you treat your car? Do you respect it and take care of it the way you would a person? It reflects back to you how you handle relationships. Even your home is a relationship. Do you keep it clean? Are you proud of its contents? Or is it cluttered and messy? That is also a reflection of your life. Do you take your money for granted and just shove it into your pocket like it doesn't matter? Or do you have a nice place to put it in like a wallet or a special place in your pocketbook? Do you make room for it? Do you appreciate having it? These are thoughts to consider when you come in contact with these possessions in your life. It does make a difference because everything you do spills into your relationships. Are you honest or do you just say what the other person wants to hear? Sometimes when we start dating, we are on our best behavior, and then after we get married, the real deal comes through and sometimes it's not that appealing. That is why it is important to start anything with the truth and not the lie that is presented to create a false sense of being. Would you rather build on a shaky lie or a strong truth? Relationships are probably the most important gift we could ever give to ourselves and others. Connections are needed before anything can work and relationships are no different. Without them, you are like a plug that stays disconnected from the right socket. So what are you waiting for? Use these tools you have read and be ready to participate in the best adventure in this lifetime. And take someone with you!!!!!

Nadia Ohar

ANGELIC GUIDANCE

When your heart is racing and filled with fear;
Always remember the good news is near;
Trust and believe and stay in the silence;
The good news comes from Divine Guidance....

Word Whisperer

Did you know that your Angels are divine messengers that want nothing but the best for you? Just because you don't see them in the "earth realm" doesn't mean they don't exist. I like to channel messages by using the "Angel Cards" that I work with because the Angels want to speak from a higher level and send you messages that will help you in your spiritual growth. I want to channel some messages today and I believe that these messages will get to the right people who need to hear what they say. I begin with quiet time as I invite the Angels to come forth and give messages that will help you grow. The first message is: "New Beginnings:" Someone is starting to venture into a new field of interest where entertaining, music, song writing, or dance is involved. Inspirational ideas are flowing to you right now and you are trying to make time for these new talents as well as trying to serve the old. There is "freedom' in the new choices at hand but you have to be willing to "let go" of what you are familiar with. You cannot see the benefits of the new until you let go of the old. You have a heart that is filled with passion and you veer away from the "serious" part of life. You like to bring in the lighter side of life and people are attracted to you because of this. You are starting to show people more of who you really are but you are still resistant to taking it all the way. Music is very important to you and lifts your spirit to greater heights. Do not be afraid to move into the world of entertainment because here you will feel uplifted and fulfilled. The Angels ask that you take time to meditate on any questions you have on your new adventure and rest assured you questions will be answered!

There's also someone out there that is ready for divine guidance and the angels want you to know that you have to claim your power in the situation you are in before you will be able to make the necessary changes that will aid in your growth. You have to set your "intention" first before you can put power behind your plan. Try not to scatter your thinking because that is what breaks up your power. Try and focus on what you intend to happen so that you can bring more balance into your life. Use music for relaxation and enjoyment because this frees up a mind that is bound tight in other thoughts. As you are emerging into a truthful place in your life, you will begin to see necessary signs that you are going in the right direction. Study that which helps you gain knowledge in the area you are interested in. Blessings are bountiful and coming your way. Be prepared to receive as you take off the limits!

There is also someone who is dealing with issues in the "friendship" department. Lately there has been drama and chaos and you are looking for the "serenity to return once again. The Angels want you to know there is harmony just around the corner and to remind you that "This too shall pass." Stay balanced in this relationship and do not take on what belongs to others. You will also need support in this crisis at hand, and just know you can ask your Angels for help when you are ready. There is a "healing" that takes place at the end of the tunnel you are going through and it will not only benefit you, but your close acquaintances also. Stay strong and be ready for peace. You are loved! Okay...one more reading:

Someone out there needs to stop talking and do more listening. The harmony you are looking for only comes in between the words you are speaking, the time when you are quiet. There is love that you are questioning whether or not to leave the relationship or stay and tough it out. All your talking will not change the other person. If you get quiet and meditate on the truth, you will find there is a 'new love" waiting on you. Take your focus off the "old" and put your energy into the "new." Archangel Michael shows up in your life to help in matters of protection and support in your "letting go" process. Decide what you "intend" to happen and then act on your decision and don't look back!

I hope those readings helped someone because they were meant for you…and you know who you are! I am so grateful for divine intervention which leads to divine resolution. Thank you Angels for taking the time to bless the people who needed to hear those messages. Thank you God for your messengers!!!!

THINK AGAIN!

Get ready...on your mark....get set......GROW!!!!

Word Whisperer

I am proud to say that I finally came up with a title for this book. That's right. "Think Again!" I think it is quite appropriate seeing as thoughts were discussed in length in this book and I also like the fact that we can re-do our thoughts at any time. It has been fun being the 'Word Whisperer" and the channel for messages to come through. There is nothing like using your gifts and talents especially because they do make a difference in this world. Never underestimate your "ripple effect" because you might never know how many people are affected by your words and thoughts. Even your "presence" has an effect on people without saying a word. It's important you don't de-value yourself because you can't help others by feeling "less than" or by putting yourself down. Your purpose should not be overshadowed by insecurity and low self-esteem. You are a person of "greatness" and it doesn't matter if someone told you differently. Go with the truth and not with the lie. Release the pain you have been holding on to for so long and let the tears flow. There is a cleansing taking place and you are just making room for the new and the good that waits on you. Start your day by telling yourself that you are loved. End your day telling yourself the same thing. You will be surprised at how much love you draw into your life by doing those simple exercises. It only takes a few seconds to say "I love you" for a lifetime of blessings! If you do nothing else but love yourself, you have done it all! This is the last chapter in this book and I am so grateful that I was able to fill these pages with a piece of myself, but also I was able to connect with you. There is the start of the "ripple effect." I hope to continue on in my work because this is where my heart is and I am so grateful that I kept going, even on the days where I thought I could do no more. Sometimes I would have the urge to "judge" some of what I had to say, but I listened well enough to know that would not serve me at all. The past is the past and the present is now! When I look at the word "present" I see where "pre" represents "before" and the word "sent" means something coming to you. I think we can only fully be present in our life after we deal with the ghost of "before" and once that is done, we are "sent" to the present to resume our life. Thank you for bearing with me when I take the words apart and find meaning. It means a lot to me to be able to use my "quirky" imagination, if only to have some fun. I am going to miss some of the challenges of writing and deciphering when I am through writing this book. This book is coming to an end and I will feel the loss of being able to connect with it every day because I looked forward to writing and experiencing the meaning of the thoughts that went down on paper. I never knew in advance what I was going to talk about and I was totally exhilarated when the thoughts would flow in and out of me as I typed away on the computer. I feel like I emptied the well and will have to find another location to get the drink I am looking for. I poured out everything I could possibly "think" of that would relate to the topics at hand and I am unloading the last of my thoughts. It really is so much easier to do a "blog" than it is to write a book. You just pick an interesting topic to write about, give yourself about 30 minutes to write it, and be on your way. Now why didn't I think of that? Anyway, I learned a lot about myself writing on the different topics in this book because I really couldn't share what I know if I didn't experience it first. Most of our learning comes from our experiences, more so than learning through books. We can relate if we have had that same type of experience. I really find the people that help other people the most, are the ones that have gone through really hard times. I try to remember that fact when I see others going through hard times, because there really is a purpose for it all. Sometimes the harder you fall, the bigger the reward in the long run. Everyone has a story to tell and if you tell the truth about it, and you don't use it for the purpose of having others feel bad for you, then you have made a difference in the lives of others. Wouldn't it be easier if we told our children when they were young that they were going to make a difference in the world? That they weren't just being sent to school to learn their "ABC's" and "Math equations" but there would be something else for them to learn that isn't taught at school. That would be to love one another, and to love self because you are your own best friend. Wherever you go, you take self with you. There is no class in school that I remember going to that taught us how to love, respect, and get along with each other.

It focused on History of days gone by or English, on labeling each word as a verb, or noun or preposition. But in my years of speaking to other people after I got out of school, no one asked me if I was speaking a noun or a verb or if I was using adjectives in my speech. I am just saying, in my opinion, sometimes school is just a distraction from living life to the fullest. It's just my opinion. But that's another book of a different color. Anyway, I want to say that it has been a pleasure journeying with you and I am excited about the new choices you will make in your life and most of all I am so proud of the "real you!" And that's the truth!!!!

SUMMARY

There's a song to be sung, a road to be driven;
A seed to be planted, a smile to be given;
A sound to be made, a word to be spoken;
A you to be loved to fix anything broken.....

Word Whisperer

It's been years since I wrote "Think Again" and my life has changed in so many ways. My children are all grown and have amazing lives of their own. My grandkids are also the light of my life and I love them dearly. When I talk about "change" and how nothing stays the same, I can tell you this is true from my own experience. I was retired and living in Connecticut in a one bedroom apartment which I felt comfortable and safe living there. After all, my family was close by and I had no interest in being in a relationship with any man because I had done quite well for many, many years without one. Besides, I used my time to grow spiritually by reading and writing and making spiritual gifts that helped others evolve and emerge in their own lives. But, the Universe has a way of making sure you get where you need to be. I eventually met a wonderful man that also grew up in Connecticut and we both had the same friends but we never met each other. He went into the Army when I was in high school so I never saw him in school and our lives took different paths. It wasn't until we would come across each other on Facebook and occasionally comment on each other's posts and eventually chat until we got to know each other better. I learned he had moved to Florida quite some time ago and he invited me down to show me around. Well if anyone really knows me they would have thought I would not have ventured out to meet someone I basically knew online. But, my Spirit knew where I belonged and my heart would not let me say no. Eventually, I moved to Florida permanently to be with him and the hard part was leaving my family and saying good-bye to start a life of my own. I will tell you this...with change comes some emotional turmoil. My body reacted to these changes and what surfaced for me was a lump on my left breast which was eventually diagnosed as breast cancer. I was not surprised because the breast represents nurturing and I was leaving my family behind. The body holds pain for you when you are not ready to deal with it and eventually will surface as some type of health issue so you can deal with what you had put on hold. The death of my mother was put on hold for me and losing my mom at a young age, I was not properly nurtured. So now I was put in a position to deal with emotions that I always ran away from. But the truth is you take the pain with you when you run. I spoke to the part of my body that had held pain for me and I let it know it could now leave because I started dealing with present and past issues. I lovingly held my inner child and allowed the tears to flow and I reassured her that I would be there for her anytime she felt afraid and I would not leave her again. I also had to deal with the feelings that came up for me that felt like I had abandoned my own children by leaving even though they were grown. It was hard but also necessary. My relationship with the man I love also improved after I dealt with abandonment issues that would send me packing my bags to go back home every time I felt insecure in the relationship. Old patterns run deep and I recognized my need to leave first before he could leave me. The reason I am sharing this with you is because I want you to see the end result if you are willing to be honest and see issues for what they are and then feel them fully!!!! They are just something to be dealt with honestly before you can let them go. I had the lump removed and lymph nodes tested and they came back cancer free. I had a pep scan done to make sure there was no cancer in other parts of my body and I was declared cancer free. However, it was suggested that I do radiation treatments and some chemotherapy to make sure the cancer won't come back. I opted not to do that kind of treatment because I am very protective over my body and truthfully, I felt like I would be poisoning my cells and tissues. I also had enough experience in the metaphysical world to know how to keep myself healthy. I keep my thoughts on love and I am quick to forgive any and all situations that arise that could cause me to lose my peace. I am happy to say I have found a Spiritual Center that practices Science of Mind principles that I have found to be instrumental in my Spiritual growth. I am also blessed to say that I am engaged to the man of my dreams and we live in a beautiful two bedroom home by the water. We will be married June 1st 2017. I thank God every day for giving me an opportunity to live my life in love and peace and continue to share these blessings with others. I just want you to be aware of the thoughts that create your life and invite you to "Think Again" if you want to make a change. Sending loving thoughts your way...... Reber AKA Word Whisperer

Starry Night Publishing

Everyone has a story...

Don't spend your life trying to get published! Don't tolerate rejection! Don't do all the work and allow the publishing companies reap the rewards!

Millions of independent authors like you, are making money, publishing their stories now. Our technological know-how will take the headaches out of getting published. Let "Starry Night Publishing.Com" take care of the hard parts, so you can focus on writing. You simply send us your Word Document and we do the rest. It really is that simple!

The big companies want to publish only "celebrity authors," not the average book-writer. It's almost impossible for first-time authors to get published today. This has led many authors to go the self-publishing route. Until recently, this was considered "vanity-publishing." You spent large sums of your money, to get twenty copies of your book, to give to relatives at Christmas, just so you could see your name on the cover. Now, however, the self-publishing industry allows authors to get published in a timely fashion, retain the rights to your work, keeping up to ninety-percent of your royalties, instead of the traditional five-percent.

We've opened up the gates, allowing you inside the world of publishing. While others charge you as much as fifteen-thousand dollars for a publishing package, we charge less than five-hundred dollars to cover copyright, ISBN, and distribution costs. Do you really want to spend all your time formatting, converting, designing a cover, and then promoting your book, because no one else will?

Our editors are professionals, able to create a top-notch book that you will be proud of. Becoming a published author is supposed to be fun, not a hassle.

At Starry Night Publishing, you submit your work, we create a professional-looking cover, a table of contents, compile your text and images into the appropriate format, convert your files for eReaders, take care of copyright information, assign an ISBN, allow you to keep one-hundred-percent of your rights, distribute your story worldwide on Amazon, Barnes & Noble and many other retailers, and write you a check for your royalties. There are no other hidden fees involved! You don't pay extra for a cover, or to keep your book in print. We promise! Everything is included! You even get a free copy of your book and unlimited half-price copies.

In four short years, we've published more than fifteen-hundred books, compared to the major publishing houses which only add an average of six new titles per year. We will publish your fiction, or non-fiction books about anything, and look forward to reading your stories and sharing them with the world.

We sincerely hope that you will join the growing Starry Night Publishing family, become a published author and gain the world-wide exposure that you deserve. You deserve to succeed. Success comes to those who make opportunities happen, not those who wait for opportunities to happen. You just have to try. Thanks for joining us on our journey.

<u>www.starrynightpublishing.com</u>

<u>www.facebook.com/starrynightpublishing/</u>

Made in United States
Orlando, FL
23 October 2022

23769541R00095